What Is Afri

What Is African American Religion?

Expanded Edition

Anthony B. Pinn

Fortress Press
Minneapolis

To Bishop William Stokes

WHAT IS AFRICAN AMERICAN RELIGION?
Expanded Edition

Copyright © 2011, 2024 Fortress Press, an imprint of 1517 Media. All rights reserved. Except for brief quotations in critical articles or reviews, no part of this book may be reproduced in any manner without prior written permission from the publisher. Email copyright@1517.media or write to Permissions, Fortress Press, PO Box 1209, Minneapolis, MN 55440-1209.

Unless otherwise identified, scripture quotations are from the New Revised Standard Version Bible, copyright © 1989 by the Division of Christian Education of the National Council of the Churches of Christ in the USA. Used by permission. All rights reserved.

Cover design: Kristin Miller
Cover art: Nan Lurie, The Messiahs, (1935 - 1943)

The Library of Congress has cataloged the first edition as follows:
LCCN: 2011015056
LC Classification: BR563.N4 P497 2011

Print ISBN: 979-8-8898-3094-8
eBook ISBN: 979-8-8898-3095-5

Contents

Preface to Second Edition

What is **Black** about *Black* religion? What is *religious* about Black *religion*? Versions of these questions have informed my work for almost thirty years, and my concern to address them in a concise way motivated the writing of this slim volume.

Developments since the initial publication of this book make all the more important such questions concerning the nature and meaning of African American religion. For example, the significant growth in Black "Nones"—those claiming no particular religious tradition—has challenged "ownership" of the theological-religious lexicon of meaning that reflects ideas and conceptual frameworks typically associated with (theistic) religious traditions. Furthermore, many forms of religious community have undergone significant changes as a consequence of Covid-19. The haunting presence of physical demise brought on by even the simple act of breathing shifted religious aesthetics and appearance through the demand for disposable masks and face shields. Some religious organizations closed as the economic toll of this pandemic made it impossible for them to function, and for others online rituals and theological commentary allowed some distance from its impact without negating completely the risk of death-dealing circumstances lurking outside places of isolation. One could worship and, say, do chores. So, what did it mean to understand space as sacred—as set apart—when it overlapped with living rooms, kitchens, parked cars, and corresponded with some rather mundane activities? Space for religious engagement became both sacred and secular in graphic and new ways—mundane *and* set apart. Did this situation change the nature of religion as practiced moving forward?

In addition, the purpose and reach of religiosity remain an open question as social justice movements such as Black Lives Matter (BLM) encourage an assessment of what religious traditions offer those who suffer most in an unjust social world. Theological assumptions about sin and personhood, for instance, fall short in light of rabid forms of racism, homophobia and other forms of injustice condemned by BLM. Could traditional religious organizations rethink themselves in light of complex social identities and fluid sexuality—and in harmony with an expansive and evolving sense of 'blackness'? How does African American religion function as an identity forming and affirming work within such a context? And what of religious communities that refuse to adjust to new framings of personhood? These are all pertinent and pressing questions that point out the complexities of religiosity within African American communities.

Still, in the twenty-first century, in a social world marked by profound challenges to individual and collective life, religion continues to matter. And, because religion still matters, exploration, as this slim volume seeks to demonstrate, of exactly what African American religion is continues to warrant our critical attention.

Preface to First Edition

So much of what takes place within the United States and within the global context is linked to religion. Both positive developments and traumatic damage in our world often depend on sensibilities and thought connected to religiosity.

In response, scholars and the general public have wrestled with the nature and meaning of religion—why it seems to matter so much to so many and how it can be responsible for, or at least linked to, activities of both devastation and development. Even aggressive critiques of religion by the "New Atheists"—figures such as Richard Dawkins—serve to highlight the tenacity of things religious. And while the New Atheists focus on religion in general terms, highlighting some rather glaring examples of religion's problematic presence in public life, others argue for the inherent value of religion as a moral and ethical compass for individual and collective activity.

In the United States perhaps no community has been more closely associated with religion as a tool for self-definition and activity then African Americans. Be it the development of early churches, various Islamic communities, African-based traditions, religious humanism, or other configurations, the grammar of religion and religious commitment seem to be defining elements of the way African Americans articulate their lives and life experiences. Whether one speaks of figures such as Maria Stewart, Henry McNeal Turner, Martin Luther King Jr., Malcolm X, Barbara Jordan, or a host of others, the public presentation of democratic life is often maintained by means of a religious posture toward the world. In short, religion matters.

This assumed geography of African American religiosity has sparked and shaped numerous articles and books, public lectures, radio as well as television interviews, and university lectures—all articulating various aspects of this connection between African Americans and religion. And all these writings and conversations have resulted in greater clarity concerning the historical development and use of religion and religious experience within African American communities. However, this corpus of work leaves unanswered central questions: What does it mean to be African American and religious in the United States? What is the nature of African American religion? Are there links between the various and competing religious traditions found in African American communities? How does one speak about and investigate what appears to be multiple manifestations of African American religion? What is *the religion* in African American religion?

Several years ago I was offered an opportunity to wrestle with these difficult questions within the context of eight lectures given as the Edward Cadbury Lecturer at the University of Birmingham in the United Kingdom. The content of those lectures was presented to a larger audience through *Terror and Triumph: The Nature of Black Religion* (2003). While composed of numerous chapters and although intentionally detailed and layered, *Terror and Triumph* is concerned primarily with five major points: (1) Understandings of African American religion guided by preoccupation with doctrine, institutions, and formal practices do not uncover religion's underlying nature and meaning; (2) African American religion at its core is a quest for complex subjectivity; (3) African American religion understood this way (as outlined in [2]) *is* religion because of its focus on deep meaning that encompasses the whole of existential and ontological concern and need; (4) Studying African American religion theorized as above requires a rethinking of methodology and source materials; and (5) Claims made within the study of African American religion must be modest because they are mindful of the inability to fully capture the elemental impulse that is religion.

These five points are those I most wanted to emphasize in that book, and I present them here in a more focused and concise manner.[1] My aim with this volume is both grand and modest.

Through these pages it is my hope readers will come to discover that African American religion in fundamental terms feels much more familiar than anticipated and seems much closer (and actually more mundane) than we want to believe. Perhaps it is at this point we recognize the making of meaning when it is most meaningful and humanity when it is at its best . . . and worse.

Acknowledgments

There are ways in which books represent a community effort. Although the person writing sits alone in front of the computer screen, she does so drawing from the insights, energy, and good wishes of family and friends. This is certainly the case with this book. I thank them all: my friends and family for kindness and good humor. I offer a special thank you to Maya Reine who read over an earlier draft of this book and offered helpful suggestions. I also remain grateful to those whose intellectual insights influenced me in writing the larger version of this book, *Terror and Triumph: The Nature of Black Religion* (Fortress Press, 2003). I continue to learn a great deal from them.

I must also thank Michael West, Susan Johnson, and the rest of the editorial team at Fortress Press for their support of this project. I began working with Fortress more than a decade ago, and I remain appreciative of the support and encouragement I receive from that Minneapolis crew.

Finally, I dedicate this book to Bishop William Stokes—a friend and advisor whose kindness to me and my students over the years is deeply appreciated.

1

Standard Mappings and Theorizing of African American Experience

What is African American religion? Really, how does one define African American religion in a way that acknowledges and wrestles with the similarities and contradictions emerging when one thinks about this question in light of a full host of traditions with a long presence within African American communities? Answering this question points in a variety of directions. Yet all these various directions draw from the historical reality of the Atlantic slave trade—the violent and widespread movement of Africans to the American hemisphere for the purpose of free labor.

It is true that an effort was initially made to use European servants and Indians as a labor force. Indentured European servants actually provided an important labor pool for colonists, although the financial benefits for servants were minor and the ability to progress socially was limited. While there were distinctions to be made between free colonists and servants, these differences were lodged in cultural, social, and economic opportunity and access—not in racial distinction. In some cases freed servants left with a trade and perhaps a bit of land, and one might assume servants would be exposed to the workings of the Christian faith. More importantly, free colonists and servants might have different levels of "refinement," but they were considered essentially of the same substance as their employers. For example, they were servants, but they were not Indians. The latter were assumed barbaric and prone to all types of despicable activities.

The "New World," as the Americas were named, was thought to be Canaan set aside for colonists. But it was not without its perils, including the "heathen" who called it home. Prior to periods of war, there was a general interest on the part of New England colonies to avoid harming Indians. In fact, colonists who did harm them often suffered legal recourse. Colonists of course assumed that their laws, based upon the word of the Christian God, superseded any laws and customs practiced by the Indians. Furthermore, regulations that on the surface protected Indians did not entail strong positive feelings toward them. Various wars waged between the Puritans and Indians testify to this. Furthermore, it was not uncommon for Indian prisoners of war and debtors to fall into the existing system of indentured servitude noted above. However, in the long run, indentured servitude proved an unreliable and costly form of labor.[1]

Whereas European servants and Indians proved problematic, hope was held out for the African slave trade as a source of an easily distinguished and capable labor force.

Historical studies of slavery clearly indicate Europeans did not invent the institution. One can go back to the Greeks and other early civilizations. Europeans during the age of exploration, however, certainly perfected its racial, psychological, and socio-political mechanics and structures. As John Hope Franklin insightfully argues, the Renaissance and the Commercial Revolution in Europe made perfecting such a long standing arrangement possible because the former ushered in a sense of freedom entailing the welfare of both the soul and body. Most profound and tragic about this freedom is the manner in which it was denied to those without means. The economic holdings necessary for this philosophical position were made available through the shift from feudalism to a town-based commerce secured through capital. While making impressive claims, a strong moral consciousness was not the hallmark of freedom and commerce emerging during the modern period. For example, Portugal and Spain decided early that African goods and bodies could play an important role in the further development of their economies and overall well-being. Hence, as early as the mid-1400s, these two countries were importing both goods and bodies, and with the exploration of the so-called "New World," the labor of Africans would only increase in value.[2] The enslavement of Africans was more than a century old when England got into the business in the 1600s.

The first Africans—also called Negroes or Negars—were brought to Virginia in 1619. And before the mid-1600s, Africans in North American colonies were few and worked under similar arrangements as European servants. It was not until England participated in the slave trade on a larger scale that Africans began to serve for life in extremely large numbers. When the Royal African Company held a monopoly on England's slave trade (1670s through the late 1680s), it transported roughly five thousand slaves per year to the English colonies.

With time and with a greater number of companies participating in the process, the number of slaves moved by England radically increased with cities such as Bristol and Liverpool accounting for more than eighteen thousand slaves transported annually. Although there were enslaved Africans in New England representing roughly 10 percent of the population by 1775, the bulk of this forced labor was on the tobacco and rice plantations of the south where slaves represented a much larger percentage of the overall population. The Carolinas were particularly aggressive in bringing slavery into the territory. For example, in 1633 colonists were given at least ten acres of land for each slave entering the colony and, within a short period of time, the number of slaves equaled that of colonists—only to grow beyond it by 1715. According to estimates, by the end of the eighteenth century there were fewer than one million slaves, but before the nineteenth century was four decades old the slave population had grown to better than two million. Although the importation of Africans was outlawed in 1808, the number of slaves had grown, with the epicenter in Virginia, to almost four million by 1860.[3]

The above figures are noteworthy, but also important is the structuring of thought that made possible this exploitation of Africans in such a systematic and sustained manner. Through a discussion of historical thought patterns, one begins to see the rationale and outline for African American religion.

Defining "Black" Bodies

Philosopher Cornel West, in *Prophesy Deliverance!: An Afro-American Revolutionary Christianity*, argues that a "normative gaze"—an ideal of beauty and values that marked the Greek physical form as superior—develops during the age of exploration. And as of the 1600s, this theory of ideal form was applied in natural history as a way of categorizing and ranking races. The closer a race was in appearance to the Greek body, the closer that race was to the ideal.

It takes little imagination to realize that Africans, defined as dark skinned, having typically thicker lips, broader noses, and more coarse hair, were far from this ideal form. By implication and based on the normative gaze, Africans were inferior in beauty to Europeans, who more closely resembled this subjective ideal. The discipline of physiognomy (used to access character from physical appearance) connected physical attributes and character by suggesting that "a beautiful face, beautiful body, beautiful nature, beautiful character, and beautiful soul were inseparable."[4] During the eighteenth century, phrenology (the reading of skulls) argued for a connection between the size of the skull and the depth of character. Although these disciplines said more about the likes and dislikes, idiosyncrasies and biases, of investigators than about humanity, such "disciplines" held sway over popular and academic attitudes. What is more, a pseudo-science such as phrenology gave these assessments philosophical and biological grounding and thereby provided an authority for racist depictions of Africans as by nature less than fully human.

While the genealogy of racism offered by West is philosophically and culturally insightful, a more historically detailed account of the development of racialism is given by historian Winthrop Jordan. Although West and Jordan may disagree on some points, they both understand racism as a modern invention. According to Jordan, ocean voyages in the modern period (beginning in roughly the mid-fifteenth century) brought the differences between groups of people into full view and fueled increased interest in making sense of these differences. For the English in particular, the recognition of Africans was made first in soft ways through literature that referred to Ethiopians, but not until the Venetian monopoly of England's foreign trade was broken after the sixteenth century did direct and rapid contact with Africans begin. English settlements in Africa beginning in 1631 and the activities of the Royal African Company, chartered in the 1670s, brought the English and Africans into close and sustained contact.

This contact did not immediately entail the description of Africans as inferior. While travelers noted difference in color, they did not frame these differences in terms of problematic sensibilities and racialized assumptions. However, this rather non-judgmental response to the African's blackness was not sustained. The English popular imagination was too loaded with negative color symbolism for non-prejudiced difference to remain the norm. Jordon concludes that, as of the eighteenth century, the African's different color was connected to a different nature that rendered the African ugly and flawed in character. So for the English, whose idea of beauty depended on paleness, Africans represented a people unattractive and with odd practices. Differentiated from the English, Africans became the "Other." They, Africans, during this period were often used as a measuring stick by which the English assessed themselves and their society, both in religious and mundane terms. At its worst, differences in appearance, social habits, and cultural production were interpreted in ways that painted Africans as barbaric and of less value.[5]

The African as a scientific, social, cultural, philosophical, and physical problem persisted and intensified as English involvement in the slave trade grew.

Black Bodies and Religion

There was a growing desire to understand the African's place in the created order in keeping with the scriptural depiction of one source or one creation, and the book of Genesis offered a theological framing fit to fulfill this desire. The story of creation in Genesis, for example, suggested a theological framework providing parameters to define the nature and character of Africans. In short, Scripture required that English Christians begin their thinking on Africans with an understanding that Africans had the same creator. A sense of shared creation, however, did not prohibit a ranking of the created order, one in which Africans were much lower than Europeans. Africans and Europeans were at least physically and culturally different, and this difference had to be accounted for.

Contained in this assertion is the groundwork for a theory of white supremacy that would take various forms. Some argued that the color of the African was a consequence of close proximity to the sun. Yet this did not hold based on the movement of Europeans into similar areas without permanent change in pigment. Furthermore, based on this argument, one would assume that taking Africans out of the sun would eventually result in a permanent shift in skin color from dark to white, the assumed natural color of humanity. But this did not happen. Such naturalistic explanations proved faulty.

Others seeking an explanation of the African's blackness turned to Scripture and found what seemed both a theologically and philosophically reasonable argument, one that buttressed the physical evidence provided by the scientific community. Genesis contained the answer within the story of Noah and the cursing of Ham through his son (9:20-22; 24-25):

"Noah, a man of the soil, was the first to plant a vineyard. He drank some of the wine and became drunk, and he lay uncovered in his tent. And Ham, the father of Canaan, saw the nakedness of his father, and told his two brothers outside. . . . When Noah awoke from his wine and knew what his youngest son had done to him, he said, 'Cursed be Canaan: lowest of slaves shall he be to his brothers.'" The failure of Africans to be beautiful, Christian, and English—or in more general terms "civilized"—was explained through this biblical story of socio-cultural difference.

It is possible, but unlikely, that a hierarchy of being could develop without the intent of degrading certain groups. But degradation is exactly what takes place with respect to enslaved Africans, and this spectrum of status was used to map out social relationships. As England's role in the "New World" and the slave trade used to meet labor demands increased, theological rationales (and "proof-texting" of biblical passages) offered useful justification for growing economic and social arrangements in the colonies. One can ask why a biblical text addressing a labor arrangement (and one not based on physiological ranking) as opposed to physiological distinctions between races was found so useful in attempting to understand the differences between Europeans and Africans. Nonetheless, regardless of how faulty contemporary readers may find the logic, the above passage held sway.

By the mid-seventeenth century, the differentiation of black bodies, with all the implied psychosocial and cultural implications, was solidified by legal restrictions and theological argument. For example, it was understood that baptism might pose a problem with respect to the black labor force: Does baptism confer humanity and brotherhood and thereby prevent perpetual bondage?

Virginia's answer came in 1667 when it was decided that "the conferring of baptisme doth not alter the condition of the person as to his bondage or freedome." Maryland's regulations governing slaves were just as strict, as evidenced by a 1663 regulation that sought to make all Africans in the colony slaves and to apply this same status to all children born to Africans at any time. Ultimately, this law failed in that it was softened to account for the freedom of black children born to white women and to free black women. Colonies further south also enacted laws to solidify the dominance of white colonists over enslaved Africans by requiring the latter to carry passes when off plantations and by giving whites permission to search Africans for passes and weapons. Georgia, which had been established as free from slavery, found it necessary to remove this restriction in 1750 and develop laws—drawn heavily from South

Carolina laws—to regulate the person and activities of enslaved Africans. Laws, or Slave Codes, in all of the slave states pointed to the same assumption: slaves were less than fully human, a form of property—both as body and labor—over which whites had clear rights that needed protection.[6]

Prior to the massive influx of slaves to North America, there seemed no real need to justify the purchase of Africans beyond character assassination and arguments of natural inferiority. While Africans often were referred to as beast-like in behavior, the notion of one creation as found in the book of Genesis prevented these depictions from going so far as to say that Africans were *completely* non-human.

This was the case until the Enlightenment, with its increased attention to the so-called scientific analysis and classification of the human as a physical being as opposed to the earlier and more theological analysis of the human as defined by relationship to God. The arguments concerning the status or nature of the African that developed in the early eighteenth century tended to revolve around the idea of the African as a different kind of human or perhaps not fully human. Although the color black was often associated with negative images of sin, this, according to historian George Fredrickson, does not suggest the enslavement of Africans was initially premised on personification of negative color symbolism. There was an economic need and a readily available source of cheap labor. Preexisting prejudices and stereotypes may not have created a desire to enslave Africans, but they certainly made this action more manageable over time.[7]

The "Making" of African Americans

While there are various layers to the slave trade—its longevity, deep destruction, and lingering consequences—slavery's power lies in the attempt to eradicate systematically the subjectivity of Africans and recreate them as objects. As such, enslaved Africans occupied a strange space in that they existed outside the recognized boundaries of human community while also being a necessary part of that same community—as a work force and as the reality against which whiteness was defined. Slaves had the physical form of the human but because of their social death possessed none of the attributes, rights, and liberties associated with being human.

Slaveholders believed that maintaining this boundary between persons and their black property was necessary to maintain their social world and avoid chaos, and this feeling only intensified when slaveholders were confronted with abolitionist demands for an end to the slave system.

The rationale against abolition was usually expressed through two competing and rather contradictory depictions of slaves. On one hand, slaves were considered dangerous, subhuman predators who would destroy white community if they were not kept in their place through force. On the other hand, slaves were described as childlike creatures that were responsible and untrustworthy but harmless if handled properly. George S. Sawyer, a slave holder from the deep south, argued that slavery is the natural state of the black and when treated properly the slave is content: "the very many instances of remarkable fidelity and attachment to their masters, a characteristic quite common among them, are founded not so much upon any high intellectual and refined sentiment of gratitude, as upon instinctive impulse, possessed to an even higher degree by some of the canine species."[8]

The nature of the slave defined by status as property is only adequate if it is also argued that the slave is not conceived as being a person in the same sense as the master. Yet the notion of the enslaved African as simply one without "legal personality" is inadequate in that laws and codes meant to restrict and punish rebellion by slaves speak to a sense of recognition of personhood within the law.[9] For example, the fear of rebellion was widespread after 1832 in part because of the uprisings led by figures such as Denmark Vesey (South Carolina, 1822) and Nat Turner (Virginia, 1831).

In addition to these plots, slaves also demonstrated rebellion on a more localized and covert manner through work slow-down, destruction of equipment, and in some cases the poisoning of masters and mistresses. Such activities were aggressively dealt with, and measures were taken to prevent such problems. These measures included night patrols by whites through which an effort was made to keep blacks from wandering around and gathering after dark. Again, such precautions imply recognition of a fundamental quest for autonomy that marks humanity.

Slaves were considered somewhat human as a pragmatic move when it benefited and helped to secure the existing social, economic, and philosophical grounding of society. This, of course, is a restricted sense of personhood in that it recognizes enslaved Africans and holds them persons socially accountable only with respect to so-called crimes that threaten the social ordering of North American life. Along with this restricted identity came restrictions on movement, independent thought, and relationships. Life became defined by prohibitions as opposed to a wide range of life options and opportunities.

The bottom line is clear: the dehumanization of Africans was not a smooth process. Although a difficult tension to hold—slaves as both property and persons—the new world enterprise came to depend on this dehumanization to stabilize and legitimize the slave trade. The questions concerning personhood and the tension between images of blacks as dangerous animals and as reliable and loyal child-like creatures took a new form after the emancipation of enslaved Africans in 1863.

Constant supervision and discipline by whites had kept blacks in line, but once free from such supervision, the southern popular imagination assumed blacks would go wild and destroy life as southern whites knew it. As one might imagine, the image of the black as a dangerous beast became a more dominant image. After the death of the slave system, the "Peculiar Institution," it no longer was necessary to justify enslavement through an appeal to the child-like and needy character of blacks. No, with the social world developed by white supremacy in jeopardy, it became important to present images of blacks as a threat.

This depiction, however, could not stand-alone. As blacks began to strengthen demands for full inclusion in society, it became necessary to present them also as bumbling fools incapable of full participation in the life of society. Whether considered a beastly threat or a relatively harmless buffoon, the dominant perspective meant a fixed identity for blacks and a primary concern with the economic gain achievable through the abuse of black bodies. In this sense, blacks remained objects of history.

People of African descent in North America experienced a rupture that affected perceptions of the world and the place of blacks in it: blacks do not make history but are the raw material others use to shape history. This is more than a historical dislocation or displacement; it is the very definition of blacks as objects. The forced recognition of this promoted a sense of dread or terror. And, as we shall see in the next chapter, this terror or dread would play a significant role in the development of what we have come to call African American religion.

2

The Shape and Purpose
of African American Religion

The dread or terror referred to at the end
of chapter 1 is profound in that it forced
enslaved Africans and free blacks to confront
helplessness, isolation from the familiar, and
submersion in absurdity. But this dread is not
restricted to the individual. It also had implications on the communal level in that it had
something to do with a despised "otherness"
attached to black individuals and the larger
black community as well. There is a tension
between individual and community with respect
to this dread.

All this prompts an important question: What
is the general response to this existential and
physically felt dread?

No doubt enslaved Africans and their descen-
dents would utilize a variety of techniques to
gain back a sense of their humanity, their physical and psychological integrity. Think in terms
of efforts to find new life options by running

away to Canada, or surrendering to current life circumstances and trying to work within the existing system to avoid further punishment. However, both of these strategies could be and were supported by a more general rethinking and re-acting of life. That is to say, dread and terror sparked and orchestrated in some cases practices, ways of thinking, and when possible institutional structures earmarked for historical struggle against (or in some cases surrender to) the terror and dread of slavery and accompanying modes of oppression.

We have come to call a long lasting model of this process of creative response *African American religion*. In short, then, African American religion involves the historically present doctrines, practices, and institutions meant to "rescue" enslaved Africans and their descendants from the terror/dread of oppression through attention to and connection with the powers guiding all existence. And it is safe to say that for most scholars of African American religion who understand the nature and meaning of religion in this way, their work is limited to obvious and theistic models of religion.

In this chapter, this understanding of religion is explored in three ways: (1) religion developed as institutional reality wrestling for liberation expressed in socioeconomic and political terms; (2) aesthetic and ritual dimensions of religion as liberation in spiritual terms; (3) religious thought as liberation in theological terms. And while my approach does not exhaust the possibilities, I must limit my conversation to only a few examples from a few religious traditions.

While terror should not be underplayed, it is important to present the manner in which blacks, through religion, at times reshaped their environment by a liberating understanding of their own agency, practiced by means of a creative ethic of liberation. The ethic generating this outlook and activity was played out on the collective level, although in imperfect and often inconsistent ways, as the sexism, homophobia, and heterosexism of most black churches demonstrates. But, while applied imperfectly, this ethic of liberation was meant to forge what might be referred to as responsible selves able to exercise agency in ways that transform existing sociopolitical structures. Such agency is important in that it forces moral accountability in a way that is appropriate only for those who are subjects of history, not objects of property.

African American Christianity: Practice and Thought

Scholars who embrace the above understanding of African American religion very often present African American Christianity (really black churches) as a prime example of religion at work. From its origins in the period of slavery, through the "invisible institution" of hush arbor meetings where enslaved Africans took the bits and pieces of the Christian Tradition received through preachers and others and reworked them in ways that addressed their particular needs, to the development of visible and organized churches of the mid-1700s, church life provided doctrines, practices, and institutions that sought to address—not always but frequently—the terror/dread of life. Through a rethinking of biblical stories, for instance, whereby African Americans read themselves into salvation history—claiming a position as part of God's chosen—spirituals, sermons, and religious doctrines were meant to give new meaning to the life circumstances of African Americans.

As churches developed some one hundred years after the first arrival of indentured black servants (and then slaves), they used their physical plants as a venue for bringing their doctrine and theological commitments to practical use by providing opportunity for thinking, strategizing, and practicing freedom. This was done on the level of individuals, but these individual attempts for change also were expressed on the communal level as well. For instance, it was assumed that, in general terms churches—Baptists, Methodists, and so on—could provide opportunities to refine personal conduct in ways that would ultimately promote liberation from systematic oppression. And it was assumed that conservative conduct on the part of church-attending black Christians would force whites to recognize blacks as worthy of full citizenship and inclusion in the social life of the country.

Beside prohibitions on personal activity, of particular interest within churches is the public presentation of African Americans in ways that reflected comportment and thereby was understood as an extension of moral and ethical conduct. Related to this point, during the period of slavery for example, enslaved Africans dressed beyond the bare essentials only when their bodies were paraded across the auction block as a way of enhancing their value for slaveholders or for other reasons of benefit to slaveholders, hence serving to extend social control over them. In response to this dehumanization through dressing and showing of black bodies, African Americans inspired by religion used celebratory dress for special events such as church services to counter popular depictions of black bodies and to soften the impact of chattel status on the carriage of the black body. This use of expressive or material culture was vital in that for enslaved blacks dress had both visual and symbolic value, drawing attention to both their individuality and participation in community. In short, whether purchased, given by whites, or produced by slaves, clothing spoke—even only momentarily—to a more liberated existence because civilization was measured and social order guarded in part through dress.[1]

If this was the case in religious services organized and controlled by whites, for the benefit of whites, it was even more important within the context of independent black religious gatherings. Hence, in black churches clothing was not a sign of one's value for others as their property but rather a sign of one's value for oneself, one's community, and one's God. Put another way, clothing did not symbolize why whites were in power but rather debunked long accepted rationales for white superiority. It was a sign of personhood and self-worth.

By means of dress or appearance—a black aesthetic of liberation, so to speak—through the donning of certain clothing with accompanying ideals and attitudes, black Christians gave expression to their humanity, to a liberated identity through the compromise of oppressive social boundaries and their supporting ideologies of white superiority. This is because through the new presentation of the black Christian's body, black Christians spoke to their value and beauty. By decorating the body in this manner, blacks forced their visibility and reshaped social space, the social environment. In this sense, the aesthetics of personal appearance as highlighted in the Black Church seeks to locate blacks and simultaneously to change the dynamics—the norms—of this setting.[2]

Tied to the proper presentation of black bodies in social settings was a concern for the proper inner health of blacks and connection with divinity. This is, in fact, yet another presentation of the body as a denouncement of the terror of dehumanization. While salvation is probably the most basic form of spiritual struggle against dehumanization and fixed identity within African American churches, there are activities and practices after this event that deserve mention. For example, many churches across denominational lines promote fasting as a way of cleansing the body and increasing the individual's sensitivity to the divine. It is considered an effective mode of spiritual renewal in that it restricts behavior by focusing attention away from carnality and the social functioning of sensuality, something that was often cited as bestial by whites and used to justify oppression.

In this regard, it is possible that centering exercises like fasting freed, so to speak, the freedom-seeking agenda of churches in subtle ways by controlling the physical body. Individual control is used to signify or twist social control. Hence, it retards over the short term the social system's ability to exercise traditional power relationships with respect to the spiritually centered black body. Fasting is not a rejection of this struggle for status. Instead, it can serve as recognition of the depth of struggle, the manner in which struggle for liberation has to do with possession of and control over a soul. Black Christians engaged in spiritual cleansing are, in a sense, taking back their "souls" with style and "grace."

Furthermore, this freedom-seeking agenda has been played out in the very worship of black Christians. Black churches as manifestations of religion respond to terror by seeking to establish blacks as agents of will, and Christian gatherings orchestrated by churches served as a ritual of "exorcism" in that they fostered a break with status as will-less objects and encouraged new forms of relationship and interaction premised upon black intentionality. The black body constructed as ugly and only of importance as a tool of labor was signified during church gatherings from the period of slavery to the present and was transformed into a ritual device through which the glory of God and the beauty of human movement were celebrated. One gets a sense of this early in the development of the "Black Church" in the form of ring shouts, a rhythmic movement of the body that must have resembled the sway and jerk of bodies associated with trances and "ecstatic" behavior in many traditional African religions.

Although despised by many church leaders because this practice reminded them of the culture of slavery and perhaps the stereotypical depictions of Africa, these ring shouts demonstrated the beauty and value of black bodies that could do more than plow fields—they could bring people into proper relationship with God by channeling the spirit of God. Such bodies had to be of profound value and worth. Through this process of the ring shout, black bodies were redeemed in ways that fought against continuing efforts to terrorize them.

When spiritual awareness is increased by means of fasting or other rituals such as the shout, the individual is open to more intimate connection with the divine in the form of shouting and possession. With the development of Pentecostalism in the late nineteenth century, particularly the founding of the largest black Pentecostal denomination in the country in 1897, the Church of God in Christ, spirit possession—church folk refer to it as being filled with the Holy Spirit or baptized in the Spirit—became an increasingly important mode of redress against rituals of reference and their consequences.

This relationship with God was evidenced by speaking in tongues (*glossolalia*)—a language unknown to the person prior to the moment of possession—as well as dancing in the spirit. The terror of fixed identity is attacked through the body's role as instrument of God's presence in the world. As so many church members say, "God doesn't make junk!" What is more, beyond addressing negative depictions of blacks, baptism in the Spirit also provided a subtle critique of sexism within black churches in that the Spirit descended on women and men without prejudice. The rules and tortures associated with dehumanization are momentarily mitigated by the Holy Spirit's presence, and the establishment of a space in which external dilemmas are held at bay and harmony is the rule.

The linking of sociopolitical and economic concerns found in the writings of many early church leaders, while not always present and not always the dominant perspective, foreshadows what would emerge in the twentieth century as the "black" social gospel. Initially concerned with bringing the gospel of Christ to bear on issues of class and poverty, black religious leaders—such as Reverdy C. Ransom of the African Methodist Episcopal Church and Adam Clayton Powell Jr. of the National Baptist Convention, U.S.A., Inc.—used this social Christianity to address issues of racism and racial uplift by arguing proper relationship with Christ required proper relationship with (and good behavior toward) other humans. In certain circles this commitment to the social gospel gave way during the civil rights struggle of the 1950s and 1960s to a more radical, black-power-influenced form of theological discourse, developed by ministers and professional theologians to address the changing nature of the church's commitment to the welfare of black Americans. This new theological discourse housed in some church communities was named *black theology.*

Gaining inspiration from Martin Luther King Jr., Malcolm X, and an informal theological discourse as old as black Christianity, black theology envisioned itself as the voice of the oppressed and the theological wing of the black progressive Christian tradition. It was a shift in theological perspective deeply embedded, according to some, in the history, culture, experience, needs, and religious tradition of blacks.

Perhaps the most radical dimension of this new theology was the ontological blackness of God advocated by James Cone. Drawing on an early tradition present in Henry McNeal Turner's 1895 proclamation "God is a Negro!," Cone in his early texts published in 1969 and 1970 argued that God is so identified with the oppressed—best represented in the United States by blacks—that God's very being is marked by blackness: God is one with those who suffer most in the United States.[3] Such a doctrine of God forces a revisiting of Christology as well. Historical manifestation of this ontologically black God is found in the god-human Christ. That is to say, black theology argued that Jesus Christ was a black messiah, a representation in human history of God's commitment to suffering humanity.

What better way to forge liberation out of a context of terror and dehumanization than to demand an understanding of liberation and justice as part of divine personality and character manifested in the faces of oppressed blacks?

In popular parlance, "black is beautiful!" While African American Christians have always understood themselves as being the "children of God," and thus being the special people of God, this theological argument is reformulated in black theology and articulated in the language of black power. With time, this notion of black power was refined through the use of Marxist social theory, by which black theology's critique of oppression and vision of liberation grew to include issues of class. Yet those involved in the struggle for liberation were reminded that social theory must inform not replace progressive action.

Although radical in nature, the theological shift suggested by Cone's proclamation of God's ontological blackness was not radical enough from the perspective of black women in the Academy. Beginning in 1979, black women doing theology and ethics insisted black theology and black churches are only true to their missions if they take seriously the experiences of black women. Liberation must include not only an end to racism and classism but also an end to sexism.

Drawing on Alice Walker's term "womanism," a new mode of theological reflection—*womanist theology*—developed and took seriously the history and cultural reality of black women as major resources for church activity and thought.[4] In addition to forcing a response to sexism within the black community and the larger society, womanist scholars have also increased sensitivity to issues of environmental racism, homophobia, and health crises such as HIV/AIDS within black communities, arguing that these evils also dehumanize.

What occurs through black and womanist theologies is a paradigm shift by which whiteness is no longer the primary symbol of humanity and connection with divinity.

Moving away from African American Christianity in the form of black churches, I provide another look at religion as historical response to terror/dread through doctrine, practices, and institutions by giving attention to practices in the form of the Nation of Islam. Disputing what it considers the Black Church's linking of liberation to further entrenchment in a system that is inherently evil and incapable of sustained change, the Nation of Islam pushed for a reconstituted black identity through promotion of a new status for blacks that rendered them godlike rulers of the universe. In its earliest and most aggressive form, this theology of special status inverted white supremacy: blacks are superior beings and whites are inferior.

The Nation of Islam

The Nation of Islam began in 1930, in Detroit, with the appearance of one called Master Fard Muhammad. Master Fard went house to house and spoke to African Americans about their true history and purpose. He disappeared in 1934 and, after some conflict over new leadership, the Honorable Elijah Muhammad replaced Master Fard and continued Fard's teachings revolving around four principles: peace, freedom, justice, and equality.

Through proper attire and carriage, the Nation of Islam seeks the respect and admiration of the larger African American community and recognition of the importance of its mission. In addition, the Nation teaches its members to maintain physical health through proper exercise and diet to counter the physical ramifications of racial discrimination on health and overall welfare.

The goal is to promote a better quality of life through obedience to divine regulations on food consumption as an important component of the practices associated with the African American's true nature. Put another way, the Nation argued some foods promote destruction of character in that those who consume them also consume the habits and characteristics of the food: "Allah taught me that this grafted animal was made for medical purposes—not for a food for the people—and that this animal destroys the beautiful appearance of its eaters. It takes away the shyness of those who eat this brazen flesh. Nature did not give the hog anything like shyness. Take a look at [whites'] immoral dress and actions; their worship of filthy songs and dances that an uncivilized animal . . . cannot even imitate."[5]

Each member is made aware of foods not to eat such as pork, collard greens, black-eyed peas, corn bread, rabbit, possum, squirrel, and catfish. The Messenger, the Honorable Elijah Muhammad, argued these foods do not promote health and should be replaced by one meal per day in the evening consisting of items such as trout, bass, salmon, beef, lamb, tomatoes, carrots, okra, eggplant, string beans, and cauliflower. Through strict food selection, particularly when combined with periodic fasting, black Muslims believed they avoided many of health dangers such as high blood pressure that plague black Americans.

Whites encouraged blacks to eat improper foods as an additional symbolization of the dehumanized status of blacks, and the Nation seeks to counter this. Furthermore, other problems such as poor self-image are avoided through a rejection of alcohol, gambling, and illicit drugs. Also, modes of entertainment promoted by the white world are rejected by members of the Nation of Islam and replaced by activities organized by the various temples including plays, documentary films dealing with Islamic issues and concerns, and museum visits.[6]

In addition to proper economic habits, modest attire for men and women, proper diet, and exercise, black Muslims were to study the Nation's teachings and develop proper relations with other black Muslims. Mr. Muhammad summarized the code for proper life through ten points: "(1) Keep up prayer; (2) Spend of what Allah (God) has given him in the cause of Truth (Islam); (3) Speak the truth regardless of circumstances; (4) Keep himself (or herself) clean, internally and externally, at all times; (5) Love his brother (or sister) believer as himself (or herself); (6) Be kind and do good to all; (7) Kill no one whom Allah has not ordered to be killed; (8) Set at liberty the captured believer; (9) Worship no God but Allah; (10) Fear no one but Allah."[7]

This code promised righteousness—the individual's consciousness resurrected and the community fortified—in that it stymies criticism of black self-sufficiency and prepares African Americans to claim their proper place in the universe through the application of proper knowledge of self. Furthermore, because information available outside the Nation of Islam is distorted and processed by whites to maintain white supremacy and to hide the true nature of black Americans, it becomes vital for the Nation to provide the elements of truth leading to freedom.

The "Supreme Wisdom" offered by the Honorable Elijah Muhammad counters the enslavement and dehumanization that mark the interaction between whites and blacks. There are three major areas covered by this "Wisdom:" (1) knowledge of the black community's history and destiny; (2) knowledge of the white community's nature and purpose; (3) knowledge of Islam as the proper religion for blacks.[8]

Master Fard's teachings as outlined by the Honorable Elijah Muhammad were clear: blacks were not only formed in the image of God but they are divine creatures meant to dominate the world. Blacks did not represent evil personified. Rather, they were good, and whites were representative of evil. Indeed, whites were considered the very personification of evil intent and daemonic desire. How else could one explain the relatively unchecked destruction perpetuated by whites?

Answering this question properly is a component of self-understanding for members of the Nation of Islam. The Nation fights the terror of dehumanization through a new theological assertion of black consciousness pointing to the damaging nature of white formulations of black identity, while asserting the superiority of blacks. The Original People, black people, in this way become the supreme subjects of history who will eventually regain control over the universe. White hegemony will be destroyed through final judgment, the earth will be purged by fire, and the Original People will rule the new earth.

Whereas African American Christianity involves an effort better to integrate blacks into the fabric of American life, the Nation of Islam rejects what it perceives as integration into a damned society. Why seek full membership in a society that is destined for destruction? Why should the Original People partner with those incapable of right living?

Clearly, civil rights and citizenship are not the ultimate goals for the Nation of Islam. Complete independence is. Furthermore, the Nation of Islam conceives of liberation as the movement of Allah over which they have no control, because Allah's actions are part of the preordained development of world events. Black Muslims must simply be true to the teachings of Allah as presented by the Honorable Elijah Muhammad and, by acquiring proper understanding of the black race, prepare themselves for their prophesied greatness.

While churches asserted equality of blacks and whites as the basis of their theology and practice, the early Nation of Islam proposed a reversal of order in which whites became inferior, barely human, and constructed for the pure purpose of committing evil acts. The Nation argued that the current condition of blacks stems from the reign of terror Allah allowed. But this was a limited period of time in preparation for the reemergence of the Original People as rulers of the world. This preparation, the teachings continued, required re-education.

Brought to North America in chains, blacks were brainwashed and robbed of their identity.

In place of healthy self-consciousness (self-understanding), slaves were force fed the Christian faith, by which their condition was justified. Some blacks, the worse type of black, not only embraced this faith but served as spokespersons for it and in that way gave full participation to the demise of their community. Why, the Nation rhetorically asks, would black people accept the religion and identity put forth by their slave masters? Can the outlook on life promoted by the holders of power do anything but reinforce their dominance? Addressing these questions the Honorable Elijah Muhammad informed followers that whites were allowed to rule for a set number of years to punish blacks for rejecting Islam and to prepare blacks for their return to glory.

This enslavement was not, as whites asserted, the natural consequence of black inferiority and white superiority. It was the result of disobedience on the part of blacks who rejected the religion of Islam. But this was a temporary situation, a period of pain and hardship allowed by Allah in order to strengthen and train blacks for their destined greatness. Blacks, according to the teachings of the Nation, maintained their specialness, their closeness to Allah, even during their period of punishment—their time in the "wilderness of North America" as the "lost" nation.

Whereas black Christians claim the favor of a spirit-God who came in human flesh through Jesus Christ, members of the Nation of Islam rejected the idea of a spirit-God and argued that God, Allah, is the Supreme Black Man who, contrary to what Christianity teaches, only exists in flesh. Only a God who is flesh could be concerned with flesh. The Christian faith developed by whites some six thousand years ago perverts the truth and teaches a reliance on a detached, spiritualized world. In essence, "the teachings of Christianity have put God out of Man into nothing (spirit). Can you imagine God without form but yet interested in our affairs who are the human beings? What glory would an immaterial God get out of a material world?"[9]

The Nation answers—there is no glory for an immaterial God in a material world; no deep connection is possible between the two. Placing a different spin on the concept of *ex nihilo* creation—creation from nothing—the Nation seeks to replace a Christian understanding of life's genesis (and its system of color symbolism) with a concern for the central importance of materiality cast in terms of blackness. In short, blackness is not the absence of something, a mode of privation; it is the color of the creative impulse.

Unlike blacks dating back to the beginning of the universe, the history of whites dates back not even seven thousand years. According to the Nation, whites were created by Yakub (or Yacub), a scientist who rebelled against Allah. This, however, was rebellion in a limited sense because it was ordained by Allah and recorded in the history of the world. That is to say, as part of the most recent cycle of history, some 6,645 years ago, Allah allowed the development of a race—the white race—that would test the Original People and would serve as their punishment for straying away from the true teachings of Allah.

One sees here a reversal of fortunes in that whites are associated with inferiority and blacks are associated with superior socio-cultural skills and abilities. Blacks, in other words, are presented in this mythology as subjects of history and whites as the objects of history, formed to serve the destiny of blacks. They, whites, are mere tools within a drama being played out.[10]

This story promotes a response to the terror of dehumanization that is not fear driven. Once African Americans recognized their true purpose and embraced the Islamic faith as outlined by Master Fard and taught by the Honorable Elijah Muhammad, they would have the knowledge of self necessary to restore order.

With the death of the Honorable Elijah Muhammad in 1975, leadership of the organization changed, as did its teachings and physical structure. But ultimately, Minister Louis Farrahkhan would revive the organization in line with Elijah Muhammad's teachings. While Farrakhan's rhetoric and often cryptic statements continue to elicit a strong reaction from some quarters, he believes the demand for divine justice necessitates the continuation of the Nation's platform because recognition of the Messengers' teachings, and the faithful execution of his platform, will facilitate healthier relations between blacks and whites. Interaction between the two will then be premised upon changed hearts and minds. But who changes?

The Honorable Elijah Muhammad's teachings contain an underlying theme of the white race's intrinsic flaw, the inevitability of their destructive activities. Minister Farrakhan seems to suggest a softening of this perspective: Can whites be "saved"? There is hope for whites who acknowledge the Messengers teachings, just as there is damnation for blacks who reject the message. According to Minister Farrakhan such a turnabout can mean regeneration and redemption. It is possible but unlikely that whites will destroy the structures and ideologies—the basis of white supremacy—that promote the dehumanization of blacks and the privileges of whiteness.

Two Examples, One Perspective

African American Christianity and the Nation of Islam, while related in certain ways, offer two distinct examples of African American religion developed within the context of African American life in the United States. The brief descriptions of particular aspects of their teaching and practices give some sense of how these traditions have developed in competing ways and to what they respond. They are doctrinally and structurally different, yet many scholars see undergirding both a similar meaning given to religion.

The descriptions I offered earlier in this chapter are consistent with the general manner in which African American religious traditions are described in current scholarship—maintaining the same assumptions and highlighting the same elements. And when one steps back and thinks about the above discussion of African American Christianity and the Nation of Islam, a general theorizing of African American religion begins to surface: *The typical theory of African American religion describes this phenomenon as originating in a historical struggle for life meaning, with liberation as its goal. Furthermore, this origin points to an understanding of African American religion as being definable in terms of doctrines, practices, and institutions utilized in this struggle.* This is the standard mapping of African American religion.

While the diversity of African American religious traditions makes it difficult for scholars in the twenty-first century to limit this theory of religion to black churches (although some try), it does not prevent a privileging of theistic traditions, nor does it prevent the theoretical assumption that African American religion points to a unique form of knowledge and experience—unique because it can be distinguished from other modalities of experience that are "secular" or without an easily identifiable metaphysical basis. It also does not prevent the assumption that to know the historical development of these various traditions—what they say and do—is to know what African American religion is. Furthermore, it is assumed that this unique modality of experience is concerned primarily with the development of liberation—an existence free from oppression, the development of a full range of life options expressed with all the privileges made available through the proper exercise of democratic sensibilities.

Although this mode of description and the underlying theory of African American religion have dominated the study of African American religion, it does not mean such an approach is problem free. In fact, the next chapter is concerned with showing the weakness of this model.

Why Standard Mappings and Theorizing Don't Work

Conversations and studies regarding African American religion have been biased toward theistic orientations. My attention in the previous chapter to black churches and the Nation of Islam—as two of the more widely analyzed and described traditions in the study of African American religion—was meant to suggest this bias by presenting the story of African American religion familiar to and accepted by most.

However, one of the strongest articulations of this bias, one highlighting black churches, comes from Joseph Washington's proclamation made several decades ago but still echoed in many contemporary discussions. He writes: "In the beginning was the black church, and the black church was with the black community, and the black church was the black community. The black church was in the beginning with the black people; all things were made through the black church, and without the black church was not anything made that was made."[1]

Based on the assumption noted above, much of the work done under the banner of the study of African American religion has been apologetic, theoretically framed by a commitment to theism, if not Christianity, as the ground of African American religion.

At times, concessions have been made to "non-Christian" realities so to speak, such as the Nation of Islam, yet the framing of African American religion effectively excludes these realities as anything more than elements external to the true focus of African American religion—the Christian faith. Even scholars whose work privileges more obscure traditions and practices are typically required to spend intellectual energy defendeding the legitimacy of these traditions as endemic to African American religious life.

Housing the Transcendent in History

From my perspective, more harrowing than depictions of African American religion as synonymous with theism or the Black Church tradition is the manner in which African American religion is often discussed as a privileged reality with special status and therefore not open to hard questioning. One often gets this perspective, for instance, from those who argue against a functional (that is, what religion *does*) definition of religion.

Harold Trulear argues against the tendency in sociology to talk in terms of African American religion as anti-racism programming. By so doing, he writes, "sociological theory has sentenced black religion in general and the black church in particular to appear in the sociological literature merely in terms of what they do, that is, how they function, without careful attention given to what they are—the nature and character of black religion itself."[2] There are implications to this line of reasoning: What is the basis of the Black Church's thought, and how do we come to know this focus?

Trulear's concern seems in keeping with the danger historian of religion Mircea Eliade saw in functionalist perspectives that are unauthentic because of a failure to recognize the essence of religion as a trans-historical "Sacred." Like some in the history of religions, Trulear pushes beyond historical considerations and frames African American religion in terms of the *mysterium tremendum* that, unlike the material stuff of religion, is not a product of human creativity's reworking of normal objects of experience.[3] African American religion becomes reducible to something outside humanity, defined in terms of transcendence and the transcendent.

The assumed degree of religious certainty associated with this position is troubling. And in agreement with Cornel West, I argue such certainty easily leads to dogmaticism that is counterproductive. It does not allow for doubt and fluidity of perspective and position—considering these dangerously close to nihilism. This is the consequence of a tendency to think of the most important element of knowledge as grounded in faith, based in transcendent claims. Maintaining this approach does not provide a language for contingencies, instead seeking to make all things theologically certain. Such dogmaticism premised on theological certainty retards human potential and limits the range of ways in which human ingenuity and responsibility can be expressed.[4]

African American religion should be understood in expansive terms that give it a depth beyond simplistic formulations. Yet even this deeper level is connected to human reality and open to investigation and interpretation. *Experience remains key.* Religious consciousness is tied to historical processes and in this way to a wrestling with the past and present in the construction of a future that is hopefully different in tone and texture. I say this because religion, in this case African American religion, stems from the terror of losing oneself, having one's very being stripped away. For Trulear, the fundamental concern is to advance an understanding of black churches that keeps intact the transcendent and that understands these organizations as tied to something super-human.[5]

Conceptualizing and then presenting African American religion as premised on transcendent reality lodged in institutions, doctrines, and practices has promoted some information important in understanding the response of African Americans to the absurd nature of life in North America. Furthermore, this particular theorizing of African American religion promoted a sense of the concrete ways by which African Americans structured their relationships with metaphysical intent and at least in part served as a way to speak to African American desire for a full existence capturing needs and desires and wrestling with the troubling existential questions of life.

The work of preeminent thinkers such as W. E. B. DuBois, Benjamin Mays, Carter Woodson, Gayraud Wilmore, James Cone, Albert Raboteau, and Katie Cannon is marked by this conceptualization of African American religion. And while the work of these figures and many others has advanced our knowledge of the cartography of African American religious experience, this theorizing is not without flaws that seriously challenge its ultimate utility.

As readers will see, I find this effort to push African American religion outside the scope of human "doing" a problematic arrangement. While the workings of black churches and other modalities of African American religion may not be simply what they do—that is, the organizations, actions, and doctrines—they are reducible to something deeply human and are the result of human need and desire.[6]

The Limits of Cultural Memory

An approach to understanding African American religion that is dependent on the historical and cultural traces of religious institutions, thought, and activity requires a trail of clues pointing toward religion. And these clues must be maintained in and expressed through the community's collective memory. While recognizing the inevitability of this arrangement, we must also acknowledge its limitations based on the fragile nature of the historical and cultural "memory" upon which a mode of description (see chapter 1) and a theory of African American religion is based.

First, double talk and signification have been vital in the preservation of African American life on a variety of levels, making possible a viable form of resistance or counter-identity. Through these devices African Americans could speak their mind, critique those with power, and not suffer negative consequences because those with power were unaware of what the wording actually meant.

Signification has a downside: African Americans have, in some cases, forgotten the "rules" to these games and have misplaced vital cultural information. Aspects of cultural memory—our

cultural connective tissue—are lost, and the stories and historical movements that have informed
and shaped religious developments are incom-
plete. In addition, much of what has been collected concerning African American culture and
cultural memory has gone through several trans-
lations before reaching print or its final form. For
example, many Works Projects Administration
(WPA) workers—paid by the government during
the Great Depression of the 1930s—who collected
very good information in the form of ex-slave
narratives were dealing with generations who had
forgotten (for many reasons) the nuances accompanying the stories they shared. Furthermore,
even when such information had been maintained, would ex-slaves and their descendants
really share all the details and the inner workings
of their lives with strangers holding tablets and
recorders simply because the request for information was politely articulated? And finally, the
context of the WPA workers, their own experiences and perceptions of the southern African
American world they entered, was unavoidably
involved in their translation and interpretation of
cultural artifacts presented to them.

Ports of memory retention and retelling can
get clogged and therefore become unstable.
Under such strain, the culture of the oppressed
often becomes "condemned to secrecy" in
order to survive, stored away in protected cor-
ners. In part what is being said here entails a

discussion of African American collective memory in "contact" with oppressive forces and the
development of tools for liberation in light of
this predicament. Such a situation poses quite
a challenge. This suggests a situation grime
but not hopeless, because collective cultural
memory is never completely lost—although the
assumptions often made by scholars concerning
the nature and meaning of African American
religion really require more than this modest
modicum of cultural memory.[7]

Contact with these limited memory-based
sources involves a type of "bringing together"
of cultural artifacts that we seek to translate
and interpret as best we can, realizing that these
artifacts never completely reveal the inner life
of blacks. Novelist Toni Morrison speaks to this
in a way that is relevant. She writes, "Memory
weighs heavily in what I write, in how I begin
and in what I find to be significant. Zora Neale
Hurston said, 'Like the dead-seeming cold rocks,
I have memories within that came out of the
material that went to make me.' These 'memories
within' are the subsoil of my work. But memories and recollections won't give me total access
to the unwritten interior life of these people."[8]

Much in the way of contemporary theorizing
and description of African American religion
fails to heed such warnings. Instead, gaps are
filled that allow for the construction of a scholarly program that seems consistent, refined,

perhaps even undeniable. Although scholarly study of African American religion is important, it appears at times to be in part based on a misuse of cultural resources because such studies fail explicitly to acknowledge that cultural memory is always fragile. As a consequence the theoretical underpinning for much of what constitutes our understanding of African American religion is less than firm.

In spite of this situation, the cultural memory of African Americans is too often taken at face value. And while not intentionally deceptive, such an assumption of structural integrity does not allow for the most "accurate" portrayal available to us. This is worth repeating: At this point, with the information available to us, the most "accurate" portrayal is not the one that covers up shortcomings and holes. Rather, it is the presentation that includes as part of its findings a recognition of gaps in knowledge and points of uncertainty that is most reflective of the nature and meaning of African American religion.

The study of African American religion must become comfortable with "slippage" in our stories and in our understanding of black life, recognizing that the available sources do not reveal everything we want to know. Perhaps in failing to provide a complete understanding, cultural memory urges us on, in subtle ways, to look more carefully and in diverse places for pieces of a community's collective story.

An offshoot of this problematic perception of cultural memory involves not only the theoretical pitfalls noted but also an uncreative approach to what constitutes proper or "reliable" source materials for description of African American religion. First lacking is the type of flexible exploration necessary to dig deeply and in unusual places for signs of the nature and meaning of African American religion.

Elements of cultural production, or "artifacts," are remnants of human activity and creativity, whether current or past, completely open to history and no longer "owned" by their creators. They are located in countless places, both obvious *and* hidden. Material culture points beyond itself to more fundamental modes of meaning and expression. Hence, it becomes much more necessary to include attention to a continuously unfolding array of cultural products in order to address the question—what is African American religion?—framing this book. Even if for the sake of argument one accepts the dominant way of depicting African American religion, there remains a methodological challenge extending beyond the theoretical crisis noted above.

Tools for the Job

This challenge to the study of African American religion should motivate attention to disciplinary tools that allow greater degrees of comfort with uncertainty and the fragile nature of cultural materials.

Archaeological investigation, for instance, provides both a metaphor for the study of African American religion and also an approach to such study. Archaeology as a metaphor and style of study might help us understand the manner in which material culture speaks to the dimensions of African American religion lodged in an oppressive environment through physical structures and physical space. For example, archaeology exposes architectural developments associated with religiosity and does so in such a way as to open to investigation the manner in which these structures speak to issues of religious identity formation because they are in fact an articulation of religious purpose. One might initially think of architectural elements such as church structures, alters, meeting halls, and so on.

But there are more examples, many of them less obvious than these. For instance, Leland Ferguson points to "clay-walled houses" and log cabins built by slaves in South Carolina and sees in these structures important stories of life forged in a new land, a life that entailed a response to their environment but one that also maintained elements of their African past. Through these structures, he argues, we learn a great deal about antebellum life for blacks. Ferguson also reflects on slave homes in Virginia.

He notes that researchers have, with great regularity, uncovered in these homes "root cellars."

One archaeologist, William Kelso, came across these cellars so often that he identified "them as a distinguishing feature of Virginia slave quarters." While commonly believed to have been a storage area for food, or perhaps just the hole left when clay was taken to build the hearth, it is also possible that these cellars housed organized activities. For example, Kelso found ceramics and other items that speak to the possibility of cultural activities taking place that slaves did not want whites to observe.[9]

Such findings should spark curiosity with regard to the secret meetings that tend to be privileged in the understanding of African American religion as growing out of hush arbor activities. That is to say, perhaps these items are the remains of religious activities—private and secretive gatherings and practices that speak to the shape and content of African American religion during a particular time period and within the context of a particular and local environment.

We typically think about these secret religious meetings in terms of wooded areas or well-guarded portions of the main living quarters of enslaved Africans. But perhaps these cellars were an alternate site for worship, for the development of spirituals, for the forging of what would become the Black Church as well as devotion to ancestors and gods associated with other religious traditions. It seems reasonable to believe that the work of archaeologists—when devoted to an understanding of the complex relations and interactions within African American communities as opposed to simply the recovery of "Africanisms"—might "unearth" information related to the shape and purpose of African American religion. The possibility alone, whether it ultimately provides hard evidence or not, should make archaeology of methodological significance.

Archaeology understood within the context of the study of African American religion offers a process of uncovering done in such a way as to maintain a creative tension between historical accounts and the undefined past. In the process it helps sort through contending interpretations and perspectives. The development of a stronger base in cultural artifacts is possible because nothing is dismissed out of hand and all findings are important in that they say something about the creativity and agency of African Americans.

The emphasis on cultural production's link to issues of humanization over against objectification remains clear in the words of Theresa Singleton, who says the following concerning the utility of archaeological inquiry: "to ignore the consequences of forced migration, enslavement, legalized discrimination, and racism misses the very essence of how African Americans created their world and responded to that of the dominant culture. African Americans did not simply adopt a world . . . nor was their world insular to those of other communities. The challenge for archaeological research is to pry open places where the material world can inform the analysis of these complexities."[10]

The archaeological approach suggested here entails suspicion regarding resource certainty and its accompanying arrogance, preferring instead to investigate everything available: written historical records, autobiographical accounts, works of fiction, music, clothing, architectural information, folk art, folktales, folklore, fieldwork related to various sites, and so on.

No Bodies in the Churches?

This attention to an archaeological approach should also make evident the importance of embodiment for theorizing and describing African American religion. What follows is a bit abstract, but it is information necessary for a proper understanding of the nature and meaning of African American religion.

Black bodies have a history and are a product of history. By this I intimate an understanding of the body as constructed (as metaphor or symbol) and as lived, as being a physiological and biochemical reality set in historical experiences.

For some this physiological form is problematic because it changes over time, therefore changing the way it is experienced. But for blacks, some things do not change. Therefore the signs of age do not lessen many ways in which society seeks to essentialize the black body as representative of a restricted existence. In addition, some might argue that the body is not a unique mode of expression in black communities.

All humans share this physiology. But this shared human physiology is not enough to negate the value of the movement of black bodies for an understanding of African American religion because, as Mary Douglas argues, this shared physical form does not produce universal symbols. Furthermore, the social system (complete with norms, language, socioeconomic and political structures and substructures) determines patterns for the presentation and function of these bodies represented in religious experience as opposition and struggle.[11] The social body and physical body act on each other, the former attempting to define the possibilities of meaning and movement for the latter. They exchange meanings through a dialectic process of pressures and restrictions. In short, the social system seeks to determine the ways in which the physical body is perceived and used.

With this in mind, African American religion could be understood to entail an effort to move beyond this exchange, beyond the pressures and restrictions of the social system. Whereas Douglas notes a type of concordance between the social and bodily expression of control, I argue for dissonance between the social body and black bodies, a discord that sparks and fuels religion as historical liberation because the former operates through a process of bad faith and with corrupt intentions.[12]

The relationship of control between the social system and the physical body is antagonistic. It is a fight by individual persons and communities for reconfiguration of the system that seeks to disembody, to use Douglas' term, interactions in ways that for blacks revolve around invisibility or being less than fully human. For African Americans, social control and bodily control (or liberation) are oppositional and adversely related. The loss of control over their bodies (on a variety of levels) was a necessary component of the social system, and structures were put in place to guarantee this loss of control, as a type of irrelevance that deforms African Americans.

The connections between these two bodies—the social and the physical—also means that freedom for black bodies must entail the restructuring of the social system. I am not suggesting that the two—the social system as body and the physical body—come apart.[13] Rather, I am suggesting that perhaps the goal of African American religion is a transformation of both through the increased freedom of the latter.

This is because the black body is not an image of society in the strict sense. Rather, the dehumanization of the black body promoted by the social system is meant to maintain the system and reflect both its wishes and fears.

Approaching the significance of embodiment—if liberation is a central concern—should involve more than structures and doctrine. It also should involve a certain style or rhythm by which the process of struggle for new status unfolds through black bodies because of the strong connection between oppression and the manipulation of the body. This is the case because so much of what has taken place for and to African Americans in North America revolves around the occupation of time and space by bodies.

Religion might just provide a way of viewing and monitoring this occupation. As Paula Cooey has argued: "As concept, 'religion' depends for its realization or substantiation upon structuring or mapping actual bodies, as well as mapping human identities as subjects represented by human bodies." The first assertion in this quotation is important: religion is a "mapping," so to speak, "of actual bodies." Perhaps there are ways in which African American religion involves reconstruction of bodies by situating them differently, presenting or visualizing blacks to themselves and to whites in new and liberated ways.[14]

Take spirit possession during charismatic church services as an example. The movement of bodies so possessed says something about a renewed humanity, a surrender of the body to a more "authentic" power, a kinetic realization of our connection to what is best about the universe. Furthermore, the proud and erect posture of members of the Nation of Islam who, through the presentation of their bodies, reject dehumanization is another example of stylized embodiment as saying something of religious significance.

Because of the pivotal role played by cultural production and images in the objectification of blacks, it is to be expected that the struggle against objectification—or the reclaiming of black bodies—should be visible within expressive and decorative culture. The arts are important because within black life they have been more than a self-indulgent process devoid of larger content.

Beginning with expressive culture, even the importance of dressing for Sunday as mentioned earlier in this volume, still a common practice in historically black denominations, speaks to a deeper sense of religiosity. The social systems restricted black bodies in that during and after slavery blacks were expected to dress and carry themselves in a way that spoke to their status. Whites expected to look at them and through their body language, the style and quality of their dress, and their overall comportment feel confident that blacks understood and accepted their lot in life. Others expressed a rejection of oppressive and dehumanizing social ordering through an embrace of bodily movement.

While dressing for church services speaks to this, so do the 1800s parades and strolls by blacks in northern cities. On Sundays, blacks moved along the streets displaying their finery, good taste, and achievements—exploring themselves through experiments with the body, decorating it, and moving it in ways that fought against the societal tendencies of the day.[15] The same type of "rethinking" of black value and humanity is expressed through the Nation of Islam's restrictions on dress.

Beyond clothing, enslaved Africans pushed toward a more liberated existence by rethinking their social and cultural context and often expressed this process in the decorative arts. Quilts and wall collages were texts full of images and patterns that spoke to a larger, freer perspective on life that Gladys-Marie Fry describes as "diaries, creating permanent but unwritten records of events large and small, of pain and loss, of triumph and tragedy in their lives. And each piece of cloth became the focal point of a remembered past."[16] This is significant because the push for a more liberated form of individual and communal life, the substance of religion as historically manifested, is discernible not only in official records of religious institutions or other easily identifiable and analyzed materials and actions. It is present also in the rather mundane materials of daily life.

These tools of daily life have been overlooked by most who are interested in African American religion. After all, what is the academic significance of a piece of cloth used to keep warm during the cold winter? In spite of this question, their value is noteworthy. While a useful resource, it must be acknowledged that very few of these quilts have survived. What this suggests is a need for additional clues in other areas of cultural production, such as modern black art. In fact, quilts and wall collages that decorated modest dwellings served as the inspiration for visual arts in the twentieth century.

Through decorative and expressive culture, black bodies were rethought, reshaped, and placed in new spaces that reminded slaves of a more liberated existence and that spoke without words to the liberation struggle waged by their descendants.

This chapter explored the importance of an understanding of religion as historical manifestation of a struggle for transformation embedded in culture. It also noted that such a depiction does not fully capture the nature and meaning of African American religion. To the contrary, African American religion is two-dimensional in nature, and what has been described so far amounts only to the first dimension, the most obvious dimension. In the next chapter, which contains even more jargon and is based on more abstract reasoning, I will make an argument for thinking about the second dimension of African American religion in terms of an underlying impulse (a deeply human impulse)—a yearning for more life meaning—that informs, defines, and shapes religious institutions, doctrines, and practices. I label this underlying impulse *the quest for complex subjectivity.*

4

Remapping and Rethinking African American Religion

Mapping and understanding the quest for complex subjectivity introduced at the end of the last chapter is of great importance for a new definition of the nature and meaning of African American religion. But before launching into that discussion, it is important to provide a few key definitions, beginning with what is meant by the term "quest."

In short, by "quest" I intend to suggest a desired movement from being a corporeal object controlled by oppressive and essentializing forces to a complex conveyer of cultural meaning, with a creative identity expressed in the world of thought and activity (that is, subjectivity). Furthermore, this subjectivity is understood as complex in that it seeks to hold in tension many ways of existing in spaces of identification—having numerous ways of understanding and expressing oneself in relationship to oneself, others, and the world—as opposed to reified notions of identity that mark dehumanization.

While some might question the religious significance of complex subjectivity, I argue it is distinguishable from other struggles for life meaning by its layered nature and comfort with both tension and paradox. For example, U.S. progressive politics is concerned with identity and identity-formation as they revolve around issues of democracy and citizenship. Liberal economic reform in the United States is concerned with identity within the realm of production or control over the means of production. The yearning for complex subjectivity differs in that it seeks to hold together, to bind together, all of these various threads of identity development in a way that makes them essential components of a larger, tangled, and all-encompassing sense of life meaning in more absolute terms.

In arguing for complex subjectivity as the center of African American religion, I am aware of thinkers, such as philosopher Lewis Gordon, who argue humans should not be understood as subject or object, or even a combination of the two. Rather, humanity is best defined by "ambiguity," a complexity and multidimensionality. Regarding this, he writes: "this ambiguity is an expression of the human being as a meaningful, multifaceted way of being that may involve contradictory interpretations, or at least equivocal ones. Such ambiguity stands not as a dilemma to be resolved, as in the case of an equivocal sentence, but as a way of living to be described."[1]

My sense of complex subjectivity is meant to maintain this multidimensional notion of being. Furthermore, this quest is not achieved in one act or in one moment in which a new status is secured. Nor does it depict a separate or distinctive element of reality. Rather, it involves an unfolding, a continuous yearning and pushing for *More*, an expanding range of life options and movements.

It must be understood that this does not entail a turn toward strict individualism. This subjectivity means individual fulfillment within the context of concern and responsibility for others. In this sense, it is the struggle to obtain meaning through a process of "becoming." *It is religious in that it addresses the search for* ultimate *meaning, and it is African American because it is shaped by and within the context of African American historical realities and cultural creations.*

Seeing Complex Subjectivity in Conversion

This theoretical turn requires some descriptive material, and for that I offer a brief exploration of conversion because of the light it sheds on the theory of African American religion proposed here. That is, conversion accounts say something of importance about the underling motivation for religion and, in this way, point to the feeling or impulse that generates religion as wrestling to develop greater life meaning.

My thesis is quite simple: conversion, made possible through elemental feeling for complex subjectivity, is based on a triadic structure of: (1) confrontation by historical identity often presented in terms of existential pain and some type of terror; (2) wrestling with the old consciousness and the possibility of regeneration; and (3) embrace of new consciousness and new modes of behavior effecting relationship with the community of believers—those who have had a similar response to elemental feeling—and the larger community.

Literary figures often have expressed the nature of conversion in clear and crisp ways that merit serious consideration. A prime example is found in novelist James Baldwin's autobiographical text titled *Go Tell It On the Mountain*. The book recounts the external challenges and inner struggles of being black in America, and being a black sinner seeking the meaning of life within community. As the book jacket argues, the book is the story of "a family in Harlem. . . . The father is an angry, eloquent storefront preacher, unable to conquer the lusts of his flesh, or truly communicate with his children; the mother, a woman of superb stoic courage in the face of the tragedies of life. The older son is a proud, bitter, doomed rebel; the younger, a sensitive boy [John] making the difficult passage to manhood, desperately searching for his own identity."[2]

This wrestling, this struggle for meaning, ultimately takes John Grimes, a fictionalized Baldwin, to the front of a small Pentecostal church and a mystical conversion experience. Near the end of the book, John is on the floor of this church, slain by the spirit of God and wrestling with the absurdity of existence as a less than fully formed human. Faced with death as the symbol of this lack of meaning, John encounters darkness and a haunting sound, one that tied his terror to a pain as old as the presence of blacks in America and exemplified by mutilated bodies. I quote at length:

> He began, for terror, to weep and moan—and this sound was swallowed up, and yet was magnified by the echoes that filled the darkness. This sound had filled John's life, so it now seemed, from the moment he had first drawn breath. . . . Yes, he had hear it all his life, but it was only now that his ears were opened to this sound that came from darkness, that could only come from darkness, that yet bore such sure witness to the glory of the light. And now in his moaning, and so far from his bleeding, his cracked-open heart. It was a sound of rage and weeping which filled the grave, rage and weeping from time set free, but bound now in eternity; rage

that had no language, weeping with no voice—
which yet spoke now, to John's startled soul, of
boundless melancholy, of the bitterest patience,
and the longest night; of the deepest water, the
strongest chains, the most cruel lash; of humility most wretched, the dungeon most absolute, of
love's bed defiled, and birth dishonored, and most
bloody, unspeakable, sudden death. Yes, the darkness hummed with murder: the body in the water,
the body in the fire, the body on the tree. John
looked down the line of these armies of darkness,
army upon army.[3]

There was a terror to this mystical conversion experience in that John's fear results from
a connection to these tortured souls. And so,
Baldwin says:

Fear was upon him, a more deadly fear than he had
ever known, as he turned and turned in the darkness, as he moaned, and stumbled, and crawled
through darkness, finding no hand, no voice,
finding no door. Who are these? Who are they?
They were the despised and rejected, the wretched
and the spat upon, the earth's off scouring; and
he was in their company, and they would swallow
up his soul. The stripes they had endured would
scar his back, their punishment would be his, their
portion his, his their humiliation, anguish, chains,
their dungeon his, their death his.[4]

John faced in the storefront church the terror
of what it means to be created a "negro," to
be a modern experiment or, as W. E. B. DuBois
phrased it, a problem—"a strange experience—

peculiar even for one who has never been anything else."[5]

John's conversion, his salvation, entailed
recognition of this history—"How does it feel
to be a problem?" to be an object of historical curiosity, an oddity—and a wrestling with it
that set him free to develop a more complex and
liberated consciousness. For John, the ability to
undertake this wrestling, to bring together the
threads of his life, spoke to the importance of
Jesus whom John saw, "for a moment only; and
the darkness, for a moment only, was filled with
alight he could not bear. Then, in a moment, he
was set free."[6] There is a new consciousness—
recognition of larger possibilities I believe is
captured in the last few lines of the novel. John,
having gone through conversion and having
been encouraged to maintain his faith speaks to
the recognition of a new direction for life, a new
sense of self to which he says: "I'm ready . . . I'm
coming. I'm on my way."[7]

In addition to accounts like Baldwin's, some
attention might be given to conversion stories
by earlier figures in the Black Church Tradition, drawn from the Fisk University collection
of conversions reported by former slaves and
published under the title *God Struck Me Dead.*

Slaves marked their humanity through an
aggressive embrace of activities that point to
their bodies as sources of personal pleasure and
social relevance extending beyond work for

others. While this served as a strike against their status as tools of labor, it also pointed, from the perspective of converts, to areas of sinfulness—a problematic engagement of the world. Hence, in conversion accounts, a rejection of life's physical pleasures such as dancing, drinking, shameful sexual activity, and so on is standard.

As former slave Charlie notes, he spent a great deal of his free time after escaping slavery in such activities, only to face the conviction that this behavior was morally offensive to God. Feeling remorse, Charlie "went into the woods and said, 'Lord, have mercy on me. I have been a sinner all my days.'" The day after this recognition of sinfulness, he attended church where "the brothers and sisters prayed around me. Then, like a flash, the power of God struck me. . . . I lay on the floor of the church. A voice said to me, 'You are no longer a sinner. Go and tell the world what I have done for you.'"[8] This encounter brought about a new consciousness and sense of self, one requiring more responsible behavior through a new way of being in the world that allowed him to have this conversation with his former owner:

When we whip dogs, we do it just because we own them. It is not because they done anything to be whipped for, but we just do it because we can. That is why you whipped me. I used to serve you, work for you, almost nurse you, and if anything had happened to you I would have fought for you, for I am a man among men. What is in me, though, is not in you. I used to drive you to church and peep through the door to see you all worship, but you ain't right yet, Marster. I love you as though you never hit me a lick, for the God I serve is a God of love, and I can't go to his kingdom with hate in my heart. . . . Whenever a man has been killed dead and made alive in Christ Jesus, he no longer feels like he did when he was a servant of the devil. Sin kills dead but the spirit of God makes alive.[9]

Charlie's conversion experience speaks to confrontation with historical objectification and the forging of a new sense of self through a feeling of personhood running contrary to old ways of being.

Past arrangements of servitude and abuse lose their ability to determine Charlie's value because God has made him "alive" and thereby open to new possibilities for individual fulfillment and relationships of equality. Charlie points to a combination of social license and the cruelty of his owner as the context within which his religious experience takes place. There is in Charlie's account a sense of trauma as the precursor to conversion experience. It involves effort to socially and psychologically escape years of slavery's abuse through strong drink and questionable conduct.

For Julia A. J. Foote, the first woman ordained a deacon in the African Methodist Episcopal

Zion Church, the trigger for conversion entails witnessing the hanging of her school teacher and what she labels her own "undeserved whipping." The hanging marked her in that "the remembrance of this scene left such an impression upon my mind that I could not sleep for many a night. As soon as I fell into a doze, I could see my teacher's head tumbling about the room as fast as it could go; I would waken with a scream, and could not be quieted until someone came and staid with me."[10]

The beating Foote received for a crime she did not commit only compounded the absurdity of the world. Foote thought of suicide as the proper response: "that night I wished over and over again that I could be hung as John Van Paten had been. In the darkness and silence, Satan came to me and told me to go to the barn and hang myself. In the morning I was fully determined to do so."[11] She did not follow through, but was left with existential angst: How could she address her lack of agency in a brutal world?

The initial response was to demonstrate agency through what Foote referred to as sin. In other words, "the experience of the last year made me quite a hardened sinner. . . . The pomp and vanities of this world began to engross my attention as they never had before."[12] Yet such activity did not satisfy her desire for a meaningful existence, for a stronger sense of being.

This, according to Foote's autobiography, only came through an encounter with religion. One Sunday as the minister preached, Foote had a conversion experience:

> As the minister dwelt with great force and power on the first clause of the text, I beheld my lost condition as I never had done before. Something within me kept saying, "Such a sinner as you are can never sing that new song." No tongue can tell the agony I suffered. I fell to the floor, unconscious, and was carried home. . . . Every converted man and woman can imagine what my feelings were. I thought God was driving me on to hell. In great terror I cried: "Lord, have mercy on me, a poor sinner!" The voice which had been crying in my ears ceased at once, and a ray of light flashed across my eyes, accompanied by a sound of far distant singing; the light grew brighter and brighter, and the singing more distinct, and soon I caught the words: "This is the new song—redeemed, redeemed!"[13]

Such a dramatic conversion was not without ramifications for conduct. Foote had a new sense of importance and meaning that required manifestation, in spite of periodic lapses into doubt concerning the reality of her new nature.

Drawing on holiness doctrine and the strength of her calling, Foote exercised her ministry. And so she proclaimed, "though I did not wish to pain any one, neither could I please any one only as I was led by the Holy Spirit. I saw, as never before, that the best men were liable to err, and that the only safe way was to fall on Christ, even though censure and reproach fell upon me for obeying his voice. Man's opinion weighed nothing with me, for my commission was from heaven, and my reward was with the Most High. I could not believe that it was a short-lived impulse or spasmodic influence that impelled me to preach."[14]

The examples of conversion I have provided from African American Christianity all have existential situations of pain, suffering, and/or injustice as a central impetus for recognizing the inner need for change, the core impulse for more meaning. One also finds a similar trigger in the conversion accounts of members of the Nation of Islam.

Readers will recall that the Nation of Islam developed during the height of the Great Migration, amid the socioeconomic disillusionment of migrants who found not opportunity and prosperity in big cities but discrimination, poor conditions, and poverty. It only makes sense, then, based on this context that the Nation's growth would result primarily from the inclusion of those angered by their existential condition. Unlike many accounts of Christian conversion that contain episodes of a mystical variety, conversion within the Nation of Islam is much more a matter of reason played out. One gets a sense of this for instance in that during the earlier years potential converts were required to think through the Nation's teachings and when ready, to draft a letter:

Dear Savior Allah, Our Deliverer:

I have attended the teachings of Islam, two or three times, as taught by one of your ministers, I believe in it. I bear witness that there is no God but Thee. And, that Muhammad is Thy Servant and Apostle. I desire to reclaim my Own. Please give me my Original name. My slave name is as follows.[15]

Only letters perfectly written, without error and in good style, were reviewed and given consideration. Once the letter was accepted, the person was admitted to membership and as a sign of this conversion an "X" replaced the surname, and this signaled the surrender of "slave" identity and the embrace of one's new, Nation of Islam identity. At this point, the sign of the "unknown"—X—marked the new identity until the Honorable Elijah Muhammad provided a new name.

As sociologist C. Eric Lincoln notes, this is only "the most outward token of rebirth. Perhaps the deepest change promised—and delivered—is the release of energies that had been buried in the old personality."[16] It is through a new consciousness—knowledge of self in the language of the Nation—that the convert is able to reject old ways of being in the world.

Conversion for members of the Nation of Islam was premised on an internal yearning for more meaning, a stronger identity than was available elsewhere. From the perspective of converts, life in the United States involved dehumanization with little hope for improvement. Trying to foster their own movement away from dehumanization only resulted in acts of frustration serving to reinforce a proscribed existence.

The ghosts of dehumanization may not be completely removed. Still, they become peripheral to the center of life meaning—or what some might refer to as the soul, the core from which meaning and behavior emerge. In this respect, conversion fosters a blooming of consciousness whereby new modalities of being are recognized and made real.

Whether described in mystical terms or as a response to historical events, conversion entails the framing of a yearning for complex subjectivity as dominating one's consciousness and energy. And this is played out in a new sense of being and a vibrant system of ethics promoting new relationships to self, others, and the world. This experience of conversion is grounded in consideration of a historical predicament—in its full array of problems and prospects—although developments resulting from conversion may have an initial tone of the transcendental.

At its worst, conversion might involve a theodicy (that is, the question "what can we say about God's justice in light of human suffering in the world?") by which converts reflect on their American heritage in ways that simply muddy important issues of responsibility, accountability, and power regarding what has happened during any number of horrific historical moments of human misery.

Redemptive suffering theodicy, the idea that collective moral evil has benefit for the sufferers either as justified punishment or as pedagogical moment, is an example. In such instances, conversion can involve mutation of religious feeling into regressive sentimentalism that reinforces narrow models of being and doing. Such narrow models in effect embrace suffering in a paradoxical fashion: as problem and as sign of righteousness. Those who theologically frame their conversion in these terms might be prone to "otherworldly" and "de-radicalized" modes of religious expression critiqued by scholars such as Gayraud Wilmore.[17]

However, conversion at its best entails the formation and acting out of a creative set of values that promote and demand behaviors tied to a strong regard for humanity and human dignity. Conversion, in this case, is an initial step toward humanity reconstituted, a loud and strong "yes!" to transformation—to the flexible reorganization of psychic, social, economic, cultural, political, geographic, and intellectual space. Writer Beverly Hall Lawrence speaks to this point when reflecting on reasons her

generation (the black baby boomers) is returning to black churches. "Now that we're nearing
middle age and are raising families," she writes,
"[baby] boomers are beginning to contemplate
the meaning of life. We are returning, therefore,
in part, because religion can provide a framework for basic questions regarding the origin,
purpose, and meaning of life."[18]

Another example given in Lawrence's book is
worth presenting before moving on. Although
well educated and relatively successful, Pam
Shaw experienced existential angst. Reflecting
on Shaw's situation, Lawrence notes,

> Longing not to be "nothing" is among the sharp-
> est hungers a human can know. It is not unlike
> the heart stab one feels in seeing one's own
> reflection fade from a lover's eye. But at times,
> even with those we know only casually—or not at
> all—this hunger not to be nothing can be just as
> crippling. To be denied a name or anything dis-
> tinguishing is amongst the most dehumanizing of
> conditions—the death of the ego. It is a common
> tool of torturers of prisoners during war and of
> slavers in robbing the spirit of their captives. The
> need to be special, to stand out, is an urge we all
> feel. . . . Most of us will mercifully never know
> loss of personhood in the extreme, but what of
> the many subtle ways in which each day we can
> be denied? The hunger gnawing at Pam Shaw by
> the mid-1980s brought her to her knees in Bethel
> African Methodist Episcopal Church. Foremost
> among her pleas: "I am somebody! Aren't I?"[19]

There is more to the impulse that gives raise to consciousness and defiance outlined by individuals such as Pam Shaw. As in order to understand African American religion as proposed here and as displayed within the context of conversion, one must take into consideration communal antecedents and historical situations.

For this I turn to work in the psychology of African American religion, particularly a modified presentation of pastoral care and pastoral theology scholar Edward Wimberly's thought because he is able to blend religious concern with the individual psyche and communal integration. According to a text coauthored with Anne Streaty Wimberly titled *Liberation and Human Wholeness: The Conversion Experience of Black People in Slavery and Freedom*, conversion experiences have a "holistic function of facilitating growth" that allowed beleaguered folks to transcend fixed forms of identity and develop more complex modalities of lived meaning as both individual and member of community.[20] Through this process, perceptions of what is real are suspended through contact with a "greater" reality often discussed in terms of a transcendent being.

While having a mystical component, this conversion process is also wed to historical reality in that it provides a space where the convert is able to reflect on and critique socioeconomic and political conditions as a basis for the development of a new consciousness. Social context can be briefly suspended through an appeal to mystical unions and visions, but it can never be escaped—nor should it. Even the meanings of mystical experience and visions are socially driven and culturally defined; metaphors, signs and symbols are less than useful without interpretation in light of history and the language of history.

The work of figures like the Wimberlys allows for sensitivity to the "shakeup in customary patterns of consciousness . . . resulted from experiences coming from sources that were extrasensory, transpersonal, transcendent, and supernatural."[21] And while the language of transcendence is not my preferred terminology, it does point to the presence of "something" that influences historical perceptions but is not consumed by these historical developments. It is a something along the lines of the impulse, yearning, or feeling described in this book as the quest for complex subjectivity.

This, by extension, affords an opportunity to examine African American religion for both its inner workings and external structures. Because of this, conversion accounts, through what amounts to an interpretative process guided by sensitivity to inner meaning, can be examined for what they say about the inner urges that inform practice, as opposed to simply concentrating on the socioeconomic and political

consequences of these inner urges. This interpretation guided by sensitivity to inner meaning can be further described as an interpretation
trained on cutting through layers of historical
"stuff" to the core of experience. It entails an
examination of events, activities, and other
realities in light of a nagging question: What is
underneath this happening?

Through this mode of interpretation we are
pushed to dig into experience to expose, as best
we can, the presence of an elemental impulse.
There is a useful shift here, a move to explore
the religious context of blacks in terms of experience of inner meaning as opposed to simple
description of religious institutions and doctrines that in fact stem from this experience of
encounter.

There is no pretense that we will learn all there
is to know about this impulse, but such thinking
does allow resistance to reduction of religion to
the historical manifestations critiqued in chapter 3. Such resistance in turn fosters attention
to the meaning of events as opposed to concern
with only the manner in which religious reality
plays out in existential terms.

What the Wimberlys say concerning the feelings that lead to conversion within the slave
and ex-slave accounts makes my point. They
too believe modes of interpretation are needed
that penetrate to the depths of the feeling mark-
ing religious life, while being cognizant of the

origin of these feelings outside "social expectations" because "genuine conversion goes beyond social expectations."[22] This is not a departure from history but instead is a wrestling through historical arrangements and structures in search of an elemental form of religion, best described not as esoteric knowledge and mystery—for religious realities limited to a few are not the essential nature of religion—but as a core impulse or feeling for complex subjectivity that informs religious institutions and doctrines of all types.

Insights gleaned from the Wimberlys should be supplemented by historian of religion Charles Long's approach to the study of religion. Doing this balances the Christian assumptions that inform the former with comparative sensibilities that oppose reliance on narrow theological concepts. In other words, a Christian apologetics lurking in the work of the Wimberlys is corrected, to our advantage, by the more critical engagement of religion expressed in Long's work. Hence, while the Wimberlys speak in terms of encounter with the Christian God drawn from Christian narratives, and what is a rather impotent theodicy, Long speaks in terms of a more general encounter with the "sacred." As we shall see, such a move gets us closer to my emphasis on recognition of the impulse or feeling for complex subjectivity as the nature of African American religion.[23]

Long's approach works from the presupposition that the sacred—the referent for religion—is manifest in the context of history and gives depth to all modalities of human consciousness and experience. Therefore, resources for the "study of religion as religion" are found embedded in cultural production and the natural environment encountered during the course of human life. It is because of these natural and historically bound objects that "sacred reality" is kept from being "merely the fantastic and the bizarre."[24] It is because of these objects and the ability of language to somewhat grasp these realities that the elemental meaning of religion can be discussed as a type of clarification, an ordering of social structures and realities or means for monitoring human experience.

Long interprets the social as experience and expression to promote clearer vision regarding issues of meaning and purpose that plague humans—a better understanding of self, or a richer self consciousness, in relationship to communal realities emerges. This involves recognition that the organization or structure of social reality is in fact an effort to communicate certain underlying impulses. Such information, in turn, helps us to live fuller lives through a critical engagement with the world because it involves "a return to the roots of human perception and reflection undertaken so that we might grasp anew and reexamine the fundamental bases of the human presence."[25] This theoretical move requires holding in tension the "position-ality" of humans in relationship to the structures, ideas, and practices interpreted.

The odd thing about history, however, is its inherent contradiction: the recording of things while promoting a type of forgetfulness. This being the case, Long helps sensitize us to that which through history we often ignore. For our purposes this means a movement beyond the obvious structures of life to the elemental structure, the impulse, motivating us to seek greater consciousness and more meaning through various modes of lived "architecture"' so to speak. It is an act of *re*membering, a rooting of structures and practices in a more central "something," acknowledging all the time that interpretive work entails coming to grips with "one's being . . . mirrored in the reality of life and history and simultaneously created in the moment of inter-pretation."[26] Hence, rather than asking about the inner struggles manifest in the process of conversion we ask how does the language of conversion speak to inner and elemental modes of reality and meaning?

When the Wimberlys' work and Long's approach are combined, we are able to ascertain better the manner in which religion should be discussed in terms of inner and less easily dis-cernable encounters with an elemental impulse. And why such discernment is vital stems from the manner in which it holds this inner "some-thing" in tension with historical structures and activities. Such a step is an important develop-ment in that it explores consciousness and his-torical action in terms of an underlying genius, the prevalent feeling or impulse as genesis of the struggle for greater life meaning broadly conceived.

Lessons from the Art World

This understanding of African American reli-gion requires the type of attention to both con-tent and form marked to some extent, I think, in art and art criticism. Put another way, inspir-ing recognition and expression of this elemental feeling or impulse is a purpose inherent in reli-gious structures and doctrines. And this is the same purpose one finds in the work of artists who challenge viewers to think beyond the con-crete presence of particular colors and shapes, to see *inner reality* as a sphere of meaning lurk-ing behind what is existentially obvious.

Think in terms of the images of celebrities or the models of brillo boxes displayed by pop artist Andy Warhol as "art." In this way, viewers are encouraged to look at items in two ways: for what they are as ordinary objects and to see beyond this to what they are as works of art. The importance of this is the question it raises: What makes something—the brillo box—art?

This query relates to the questions underlying my critique in chapter 3 and the theory of religion promoted in this chapter: What makes something religiously significant? What makes something religion? Is there more to historical structures than what readily meets the eye? Such questions train students of religion, in this case African American religion, to approach materials with sensitivity to the links between content and form, identity and aesthetics.

Seeing involves more than what meets the eye because it requires recognizing the deep value of what visual realities do not give up right away but rather present as opaque influences. In like manner, art holds in tension material existence and non-material impulses (the motivation and meaning underneath the artwork), and it brings to the mind of the viewer the presence of this non-material impulse in ways that impact relationships with historical realities and materials. Art has the ability to affect us by drawing out into the open concealed realities, possibilities, and meanings thereby teaching us connections between historical developments and inner urges.

Or as Hilton Als, staff writer for *The New Yorker* magazine, remarks, "the art that affects us and attacks us with the artist's passion and dreams is something we've seen before, somewhere, if only we could place it. It's a matter of how deeply one has ever looked at one's interior world: it's been there all along."[27] Content and form, material history and elemental impulses, bleed into each other. Art so conceived points to an underlying reality, and by extension art criticism sheds light on how to discuss and explore elemental reality and its relationship to the historical material through which it is manifest.

Questioning art, so to speak, requires attention to both the visual dimensions of all art as well as the manner in which it signifies nonmaterial realities. In this way, remaining mindful of both content and form allows for the exploration of connected concerns: what art is and what it means or signifies as well as how it is made, its history of production. Those who undertake this exploration, according to philosopher of art Arthur Danto, are involved in art criticism because addressing content and form without segregating one from the other is not only possible but also plausible, and "putting all that into words is what art criticism is."[28] Weaving together content and form—and art should have both—requires a type of patient examination, a sustained looking at and looking to.

This is the important point drawn from what I have said about art: thinking about the work of art criticism offers a way of thinking about religion as the quest for complex subjectivity. It provides a means by which to wrap one's mind around this idea of religion as more than meets the eye. As such, I hope seeing art and discussions of art related to the hidden within the obvious makes what I have suggested concerning religion appear less odd and more manageable regardless of one's personal commitments. And I want to be certain this chapter ends by taking readers back to the starting point—the basic point of concern.

Complex Subjectivity and Right Behavior

African American religion at its core is the quest for complex subjectivity, a desire or feeling for more life meaning. In other words, African American religion's basic structure entails a push or feeling for "fullness" of life. And this central concern for subjectivity that is African American religion is not limited to a particular "tradition." Therefore, this basic structure or primary impulse accounts for the Christian's talk of connection to the image of God in ways that subvert (at times and at other times support) racist/sexist depictions of blacks as inferior beings. It accounts for the Nation of Islam's proclamation of the black person as "god," with the positive and negative ramifications of this proclamation. This impulse also undergirds recognition of the human's connection to divine powers found in traditions such as Voodoo as well as the strong attention to humanity found in religious humanism and does so in a way that points to both the benefits and flaws within these systems. It encompasses all these examples—both the positive and negative dimensions of these examples.

Complex subjectivity stands for a healthy self-concept that requires adherence to the privileges and responsibilities associated with those who shape history. It is the creative struggle in history for increased agency. Religious experience thus entails a human response to a crisis of identity. In some regards, this religious experience may be described as a form of mystical experience, a type of transforming experience that speaks to a deeper reality, guided perhaps by a form of esoteric knowledge. Nonetheless, I argue that even this depiction often presented in terms of "hidden symbols and obscure signs" ultimately points back to this yearning for complex subjectivity. And it is conditioned by culture and thereby related to history.

I cannot conclude without giving some attention to the system of ethics accompanying my understanding of African American religion. Regarding this system, I suggest a reciprocal relationship between our creative impulses expressed in culture and the activities we consider appropriate and "right": we are "moved" to behave in certain ways, to value certain interactions and to disregard others.

Mindful of my attention to art in this chapter, I venture to say understanding cultural production teaches lessons concerning values, choices, and power that can move us ethically. So as not to give the impression that aesthetic experience is always considered positive, let me qualify my assertion by saying that at the very least interaction with cultural production forces a confrontation with ethics and moral sensibilities: What does a song, painting, novel, style of dress say to us? What behavior does it inspire or dissuade? In what remains of this chapter, my goal is to present a response to these questions, one revolving around what I will call an *ethics of perpetual rebellion.*

Within this system of ethics is a continuing concern with movement away from dehumanization, but it is understood that struggle may not provide the desired results. However, in place of this outcome-driven system, my proposed ethical outlook locates success in the process. We continue to work toward "liberation" and maintain this effort because we have the potential to effect change, measuring the value of our work not in the product but in the process of struggle itself.

I am in agreement with ethicist Sharon Welch. There is no foundation for moral action that guarantees individuals and groups will act in "productive" and liberating ways nor that they will ultimately achieve their objectives. Therefore, ethical activity is risky or dangerous because it requires operating without the certainty and security of a clearly articulated "product."[29] Ethics in this sense is a commitment to rebellion, a rejection of oppressive identities, and an endless process of struggle for something more. There is no certainty, no way of knowing our efforts will have long-term benefits or sustained merit. But this is not the point.

In this system of ethics, the goal of social activism, or struggle, is the fostering of space, broadly defined, in which we can undertake the continual process of rethinking ourselves in light of community and within the context of the world. Through this process at its best, we chip away at the structures of dehumanization and in their place foster the formation of transformative possibilities. But at other times, our actions reinforce these structures of dehumanization. In other words, "we are" as Stuart Hall remarks, "always in negotiation, not with a single set of oppositions that place us always in the same relation to others, but with a series of different positionalities. Each has for us its point of profound subjective identification."[30]

5

A New Theory of African American Religion

Is This Experience Religious?

What I outlined in chapters 1 and 2 and critiqued in chapter 3 entails a historically and culturally determined sense of religion that is known through structures and practices. But this is only one dimension of African American religion, and if this were the end, one might think it could not exist without the process of dehumanization: no dehumanization, no need for liberation-focused activity. But as I argued in chapter 4, there is a deeper, elemental impulse, an inner stirring that actually informs and shapes African American religion. This impulse is known or understood in part through historical manifestation, *but* this "feeling" exists prior to these manifestations and informs these historically situated practices and beliefs.

This feeling, which underlies institutional and doctrinal manifestations of African American religion, is a creative impulse that would be present regardless of historical circumstances. This is because the human makeup allows for continual transformation, and humans desire life-meaning that evolves and grows, that is not restricted to situations of overt oppression. Religion would persist regardless of historical circumstances, to borrow a statement from historian of religion Mircea Eliade, because humans "thirst for being," and any number of things beyond white supremacy or sexism could provide context for satisfying this thirst and the celebration of consequential growth when it occurs.[1]

Having a sense of what religion is on a fundamental level is only half the battle. The next challenge is to develop a way of exploring religion so conceived. Or in the formation of a question: How should those involved in the study of African American religion make sense of this quest and its ramifications?

Experiencing Religion

Void of interpretation, religious experience as described in the previous chapter—represented by conversion—is little more than psychological moans and groans lacking clarity and decipherable importance. In this sense, to play on philosopher of religion Wayne Proudfoot's argument, religious experience cannot be known unless it can be interpreted and cannot be interpreted unless there are real connections to a social context and practices that have formative consequences for the meaning of the experience.[2] Here is that troublesome word, used liberally in this book—"experience." But what does it mean? What is experience? And what is religious experience?

One might say that religious experience is any encounter that the person involved considers religious. I think there is something to this—the person's history and description of his or her encounter is important information. But I think that type of description can lack a necessary critical component if it handcuffs discussion by and critique from others. Too insular a process has its problems. While members of a given religious community should see themselves and their religious worldview expressed in any description of conversion or religious practice, it is unnecessary and potentially damaging to limit critical analysis to comments members of that community find acceptable on an explanatory level.

Still others might argue that religious experience is that which cannot be reduced to natural occurrences or explanation in that it entails an encounter with the sacred—a "something" outside the realm of human understanding. I have already rejected such a definition through my argument for religion as determined by social and cultural environments and developments.

While it is unlikely that I can suggest a definition for religious experience that will satisfy most, *I would like to define religious experience, in the context of black America, as the recognition of and response to the elemental feeling for complex subjectivity and the accompanying transformation of consciousness that allows for the historically manifest battle against the terror of fixed identity.*

While this experience likely won't result in sustained socio-political and cultural transformation, it does involve a new life meaning that encourages continued struggle for a more robust existence. This process is not limited to the individual but also entails community; new consciousness and struggle for life meaning from fixed identity requires connection to and work with others. And the flipside of this, when African American religion actually involves destructive behaviors and practices, also involves connection to and work with others.

A consideration of the dilemma between experiencing African American religion and explaining it remains. Like philosopher of religion Wayne Proudfoot and historian of religion Ann Taves, I want to keep these two in creative tension.[3] The argument made thus far would suggest that history is not ignored in African American religious experience. Rather, it is wrestled in ways that promote new possibilities of being. Hence, turning once again to conversion experience, there is, according to psychologist of religion Edward Wimberly, a basic structure attested to by slaves and post-slavery African Americans that "precipitated a radical turnaround in thinking and behavior which became nurtured and acted out in Christian community."[4]

Although discussed by Wimberly in terms of the Judeo-Christian tradition, the work of religious experience outlined is certainly relevant to other traditions present in African American communities. Religious experience within any number of traditions (both theistic and non-theistic) entails meaning that comes "as a result of reshaping the past according to present experiences."[5]

The impulse or feeling for complex subjectivity is present at least in soft tones in each person. And a particular arrangement of historical circumstances experienced in a particular way sensitizes some to this feeling in ways others do not encounter. While I want to state clearly that this religious experience can lead to involvement in a variety of traditions—some less well known and of questionable status within the study of religion and popular opinion (such as humanism)—I want to hold in tension as a real possibility the "nonreligious" person. In this way porous parameters are established around the "religious" in ways that add some clarity to its definition while also recognizing that not all understand themselves as operating out of this impulse. This is certainly the case for African American secular atheists, of which there are more than a few.[6]

The possibility of the "non-religious" person raises questions that should be addressed, for example: Is the impulse inherently human if some deny motivation based on it? Such questions will shed additional light on the nature and meaning of religion. But I must give this additional thought and therefore be rather tentative in my statements. At this stage, I propose that not every person desires to speak of a religious experience, recognition of and response out of the inner impulse. And it should be added that the non-religious, such as secular atheists, feel no loss in not claiming religious experience as a primary orientation. They may be able to outline the inspired embrace of a particular political platform, economic system and philosophy, or cultural formation.

These may be said to constitute life-changing experiences. But they alone do not constitute the transformation of total being, the constitution of a new consciousness that sparks new meanings of a life endemic to religion as feeling for complex subjectivity and religion as historical manifestation of this feeling in the form of institutions, doctrines, and practices.

Finally, regarding those for whom religious experience is a fitting conceptual framework, there is an unavoidable question: Even if the presence of this impulse is acknowledged, why consider it religion?

This impulse constitutes the basis of African American religion because of the wide-ranging and far-reaching goal associated with it. Again, sociopolitical and psychological health is only one of the dimensions of this commitment and the space in which this "wholeness" develops. There is also an element that is not definable in those terms, a component not fully understood. It is this continual unfolding of newly recognized dimensions of our thinking and "be-ing" that pushes this sense of religion beyond the level of philosophy or community activism. It entails recognition of levels of being reflected in sociopolitical circumstances but not fully captured through these circumstances. It involves more than just a correction of material inequality, more than political struggle, because it is concerned with the very meaning of life. This impulse is larger, more expansive, and addresses the very nature of our existence in ways that *tie or bind* together historical struggles with basic needs and desires that cut to our very core.

This impulse, a type of deep stirring that I define as the elemental nature of African American religion, is the framework for a world system, a new way of conceiving of the wholeness of being that cannot be contained in schemes of meaning premised merely upon the acquisition of rights as payment for the historical workings of white supremacy. A new world system, of course, has implications for any and all who are willing to fall under its sway. And in this sense, it has the potential to involve a new way of being, a new mode of meaning that effects more than those with black skin.

African American religion, then, is not a transhistorical mode of reality but rather a creative and bold wrestling with history in order to place African American bodies in healthier spaces, with a greater range of possibilities. It is a deeply human enterprise—involving both the physicality of human life and the deeper desires embedded in humanity's materiality.

What are the implications of this statement? For example, does it mean the gods and their stories are illusions, figments of our imagination?

No, not in the way that, say, secular humanists might suggest. The language used by the oppressed in developing their stories has a materiality of its own that renders the gods "true." In pragmatic terms, *they are real and present to believers*, and this gives them a certain type of functional validity. However, drawing from the work of historians of religions, I argue that gods are mythic—as opposed to fictitious—figures whose stories and rites explain something about the core feelings revolving around subjectivity and who provide examples of how to extend agency in beneficial (and sometimes harmful) ways. Hence, gods, spirits, and the like that inhabit religious doctrine and stories model ways of being in the world, modalities from which members of a given tradition are able to draw in the development of their own consciousness.[7] Put another way, the gods are cultural constructs, "matters" of cultural worlds, and as such they have a certain type of reality.

This is why some can bring into fundamental question god or gods—relying instead on the fragile but real sense of human potential. But more to the point, this is the reason why African American Christians talk in terms of being followers of Christ and why members of the Nation of Islam discipline themselves to embrace the model of agency presented by the Honorable Elijah Muhammad, the Christ figure for the modern age. It is why being the "son" or "daughter" of a particular *orisha* or god says something about the characteristics or talents of practitioners of santería. Accordingly, the gods and other divine beings, through their actions and words, point to modes of consciousness that imply *more*—more possibilities, more complexity, and more vitality. *More.*

How to Study African American Religion

What I have argued up to this point begs the question: How does one undertake the study of African American religion as the quest for complex subjectivity?

The theorizing of African American religion as quest for complex subjectivity is a tool for thinking about religion for professionals (scholars, religious leaders, and so on) and for "laypersons." Thinking clearly and deeply about religious worlds is beneficial regardless of one's professional commitments or personal relationship to religiosity. Such clarity helps make sense of sociopolitical, economic, and cultural developments felt with passion and helps shed light on the fundamental yearning that guides the ways in which people approach others and the world. Who wouldn't gain something through greater clarity concerning what underlies thought and action?

The value of this deep thinking on the nature and meaning of religion is somewhat obvious. The need for a proper method for studying religion so conceived is a more specialized need. I recognize not everyone has the need for this type of investigation. Knowing a more robust definition of religion is sufficient for most—one that can be applied to their local situation and can be used to interpret national and global developments as they read the paper, talk to friends, and so on. But for those who need or want more, this section offers a creative method for studying African American religion.

The method I propose is *relational central-ism.* It is an interdisciplinary method of study combining insights from psychology of reli-gion's work on conversion, history of religions, sociology of religion, theological analysis, and art criticism through which the relationship or resemblance between modes of African Ameri-can religion is explored in terms of their shared referent. Relational centralism helps decipher patterns and layers of meaning and movement in order to put in perspective the past, present, and future possibilities for more fulfilled exis-tence. This approach fosters recognition of deep commonality between groups–the elemental nature of all religious experience–that links us while also recognizing the important differences between various religious traditions.

We can observe a healthy tension between the distinctive manner in which religion oper-ates within particular historical moments and the common impulse undergirding all historical manifestations of African American religion. I refer to this approach as *relational* centralism because of this attention to both particularity and the shared impulse that marks all humans.

As an approach to the study of African American religion, relational centralism oper-ates based on a set of theoretical assumptions and interpretative questions, both of which serve not only to collect and observe resources for evaluation but also to analyze these resources. The questions sharpen focus and clarify the "shape" of religiosity so conceived. And the basic assumptions help to contextualize study through the formation of an appropriate vocabulary for naming the religious as well as through promoting awareness of nuance and detail.

Five Assumptions

First, utilizing this approach requires an understanding that the self, community, and the world constructed by humans all serve as resources for study. Attention to religious institutions, doctrines, and other historically situated realities does not assume them to be insular. But they are important because they entail encounter with the manifestations of a deeper "something." Therefore, they reveal more than just a particular moment in human history and social interaction. Such a study reveals, as historians of religions might note, realities hidden from "immediate experience."[8]

Second, this underlying "something" is best described as an impulse or feeling for complex subjectivity that is, through attention to its rupturing of historical situations, open to investigation.

Third, one must also recognize that this feeling or impulse is the genius behind all forms of African American religious practice.

Fourth, relational centralism requires an assumption that better understanding this underlying impulse and how it operates will also generate better knowledge of what it means to be human in terms not restricted to race.

Finally, this approach requires realism (measured optimism) with respect to projected outcomes of study, recognizing that religion as elemental impulse cannot be fully captured by the exploratory tools available to us.

These theoretical assumptions when taken together urge methodological humility along the lines of what Arnold Hauser says about art criticism: "Works of art [are] like unattainable heights. We do not go straight towards them, but circle round them."[9] Again, as a consequence, we must think about religion's core, the feeling for complex subjectivity, as entailing movement toward "*more*," a term I used at the end of the last section to designate a continual unfolding of meaning.

While being accessible through historical realities that generate high potential for deeper understanding, this does not entail full comprehension of this quest for complex subjectivity. Limitations of this kind are not a problem but a necessity, in part because this method aims to clarify the nature and meaning of religion while recognizing that such clarification must also mean a persistent uncertainty. Perhaps this is why historians of religion often talk about religion in terms of opacity and define the study of religion as an oblique process that "provides us with hints that remain too fragile to bear the burden of being solutions."[10]

Questions

Guided by interdisciplinary sensibilities, relational centralism poses questions revolving around a concern with the extraction of meaning. Applying these questions helps to unpack African American religion in ways that make more evident its core values and concerns. The first question seeks to pull away layers of history to expose the internal impulse by asking: *Can the present reality be reduced to a common denominator, or does the reality point to itself as the genius of African American religion?*

So when applied to African American churches or the Nation of Islam, for example, the answer must be no, because both religious organizations can be reduced to individuals who have had a certain "encounter" and as a consequence construct buildings and develop doctrines. And this can be reduced further to a source for this encounter. When the first question is applied, it forces a move through historical developments to the source of these developments. By so doing, the importance of both the historical (or external) and the elemental impulse (or center) are considered. Or in other words, it promotes a productive tension between what might resemble historian of religions Jonathan Z. Smith's interpretation as a "centripetal" view and "centrifugal" view by which both the center and periphery of religious life are valued.[11]

Using this approach also requires sensitivity to comparison as an element of interpretation. And so the next several questions will be:

- What is to be made of the various incarnations of the elemental nature of religion?

- Does the arrangement of African American life and its priorities point to the "texture" of this elemental yearning?

- Do the diverse manifestations and the context of each manifestation say something about the nature of this elemental impulse?

- Do similarities and differences in modalities of manifestation point to particular attributes and characteristics of this impulse?

These questions appeal to the relational nature of this approach by seeking to put in better focus our understanding of what is religious about African American religion through a framework of analogy.

Comparison in itself, however, is far from enough. The generalizations on which comparison is based do not provide focused insights, and some comparisons are awkward at best, based as they are on the limits of our theoretical language. For example, to say that manifestations of religion in African American contexts share a concern with worship is partially useful in that it might point to the manner in which the body figures in religious practice. But it shows a bias toward particular modes of religious expression—talk of worship is a poor fit with many humanist communities as well as the Nation of Islam. Furthermore, only an extremely loose definition of sacred text as a mode of expressing the elemental nature of African American religion can make it applicable for analogy between traditions such as churches and traditions in African American communities that are more oral in orientation (that is, Yoruba-based traditions).

In any case, the comparative component of the approach I suggest here runs the risk of ranking traditions as "superior" and "inferior" based upon the categories used to undertake the analogy. Being mindful of this, relational centralism is concerned with uncovering dimensions of religion's elemental impulse while seeking to hold in tension value judgments based on the interpreter's own cultural sensibilities and commitments. Such judgments are useless because no one cultural product through which the elemental nature of religion emanates is more "sacred," to use popular terminology, than another. As historians of religions have argued, manifestation of the sacred is a situational affair that is flexible and subject to change based on historical need and materials available. In this sense religion's features are much more ordinary than extraordinary.[12]

I end this chapter and the book by restating the hope that concluded the preface. Through a reevaluation of African American religion's nature and meaning, we may come to discover that African American religion in fundamental terms feels much more familiar than anticipated and seems much closer than one might want to believe. Perhaps at this point we recognize the making of meaning when it is most meaningful, and humanity when it is at its best . . . and worse.

Notes

Preface to First Edition

1. In order to make this volume "reader friendly," I have removed many of the direct quotations and extended footnotes related to the ideas presented. I do provide references when they are most essential, particularly when explicating ideas and themes that grow out of my reading of related scholars. However, readers interested in the full footnote materials should see the corresponding themes and ideas as they are fully presented in *Terror and Triumph* (Minneapolis: Fortress Press, 2003).

Chapter 1: Standard Mappings and Theorizing of African American Experience

1. Alden T. Vaughan, *New England Frontier: Puritans ad Indians, 1620–1675* (Boston: Little, Brown and Company, 1965), 96, 186, 207.

2. John Hope Franklin, *From Slavery to Freedom: A History of Negro Americans*, 5th ed. (New York: Knopf, 1980), 31.

3. Rondal Segal, *The Black Diaspora: Five Centuries of the Black Experience outside Africa* (New York: Farrar, Straus & Giroux, 1995), 22–23; Franklin, *From Slavery to Freedom*, 58, 132.

4. Cornel West, *Prophesy Deliverance! An Afro-American Revolutionary Christianity* (Philadelphia: Westminster, 1982), 58.

5. Winthrop D. Jordan, *White Over Black: American Attitudes toward the Negro, 1550–1812* (Chapel Hill: University of North Carolina Press, 1968), 5–8, 22–25, 40–43.

6. Franklin, *From Slavery to Freedom*, 54–55, 56–58.

7. Jordan, *White Over Black*, 28; George M. Fredrickson, *White Supremacy: A Comparative Study in American and South African History* (New York: Oxford University Press, 1981), 70–74, 191.

8. Fredrickson, *The Black Image in the White Mind: The Debate on Afro-American Character and Destiny, 1817–1914* (New York: Harper & Row, 1971), 54–57; Orlando Patterson, *Slavery and Social Death: A Comparative Study* (Cambridge: Harvard University Press, 1982), 22.

9. Orlando Patterson, *Slavery and Social Death: A Comparative Study* (Cambridge: Harvard University Press, 1982), 22.

Chapter 2: The Shape and Purpose of African American Religion

1. Shane White and Graham White, *Stylin': African American Expressive Culture, from Its Beginnings to the Zoot Suit* (Ithaca: Cornell University Press, 1999), 127; Helen Bradley Foster, *"New Raiments of Self": African American Clothing in the Antebellum South* (New York: Berg, 1997), 2–4.

2. Linda B. Arthur, introduction to *Undressing Religion: Commitment and Conversion from a Cross-Cultural Perspective* (New York: Berg/Oxford International, 2000), 2–3.

3. James H. Cone, "Preface to the 1989 Edition," in *Black Theology and Black Power* (1969; reprint, San Francisco: Harper & Row, 1989), vii.

4. Alice Walker, *In Search of Our Mothers' Gardens* (San Diego: Harcourt Brace Jovanovich, 1983).

5. Elijah Muhammad, *How to Eat to Live, Book No. 1* (Atlanta: M.E.M.P.S. Publications, 1967), 14.

6. Ibid., 17, 102.

7. Elijah Muhammad, *The Supreme Wisdom* (Hampton: United Brothers and U.S. Communications Systems, n.d.), 52–53.

8. Elijah Muhammad, *The Fall of America* (Chicago: Muhammad's Temple of Islam No. 2, 1973), 3.

9. Muhammad, *Supreme Wisdom*, 9.

10. Malcolm X, *Yacub's History* (Stone Mountain: T.U.T. Publications, 1997); Malcolm X, *The End of White World Supremacy: Four Speeches by Malcolm X* (New York: Arcade, 1971), 23–66.

Chapter 3: Why Standard Mappings and Theorizing Don't Work

1. Joseph Washington, "How Black Is Black Religion?" in James J. Gardiner and J. Deotis Roberts Sr., eds., *Quest for a Black Theology* (Philadelphia: Pilgrim, 1971; reprint, Minneapolis: Fortress Press, 2010), 28.

2. Harold Dean Trulear, "A Critique of Functionalism: Toward a More Holistic Sociology of Afro-American Religion," *Journal of Religious Thought* 42:1 (Spring 1985): 39.

3. Mircea Eliade, *Patterns in Comparative Religion* (New York: Meridian, 1958); Mircea Eliade, *The Sacred and the Profane: The Nature of Religion* (New York: Harvest, 1959); Robert G. Hamerton-Kelly, ed., *Violent Origins: Walter Burkert, René Girard, and Jonathan Z. Smith on Ritual Killing and Cultural Formation* (Stanford: Stanford University Press, 1987), 4–5.

4. Cornel West, "The Historicist Turn in Philosophy of Religion," in *The Cornel West Reader* (New York: Basic Civitas, 1999), 360–67.

5. Trulear, "A Critique of Functionalism," 38–50.

6. Understand this statement over against Trulear's reading of African American religion in "A Critique of Functionalism," 38–50.

7. Pierre Nora, "Between Memory and History: Les Lieux de Memoire," in Geneviene Fabre and Robert O'Meally, eds., *History and Memory in African-American Culture* (New York: Oxford University Press, 1994); 284; Frantz Fanon, *Black Skin, White Masks* (New York: Grove, 1967), 237.

8. Toni Morrison, "The Site of Memory," in Russell Ferguson et al., eds., *Out There: Marginalization and Contemporary Cultures* (Cambridge: MIT Press, 1990), 302.

9. Leland Ferguson, *Uncommon Ground: Archaeology and Early African America, 1650–1800* (Washington, D.C.: Smithsonian Institution Press, 1992), xliv, 58; Theresa A. Singleton, ed., *"I, Too, Am America": Archaeological Studies of African-American Life* (Charlottesville: University of Virginia Press, 1996), 5.

10. Singleton, *"I, Too, Am America,"* 17.

11. Mary Douglas, *Natural Symbols: Explorations in Cosmology* (New York: Routledge, 1996), 67–69; Mary Douglas, *Purity and Danger: An Analysis of the Concepts of Pollution and Taboo* (New York: Ark, 1966).

12. Mary Douglas, *Natural Symbols*, 67–69.

13. Ibid.

14. Paula Cooey, *Religious Imagination and the Body: A Feminist Analysis* (New York: Oxford University Press, 1991), 110.

15. Shane White and Graham White. *Stylin': African American Expressive Culture, from Its Beginnings to the Zoot Suit* (Ithaca: Cornell University Press, 1998), 94, 84, 154, 176.

16. Gladys-Marie Fry, *Stitched from the Soul: Slave Quilts from the Ante-bellum South* (New York: Dutton Studio, 1990), 1.

Chapter 4: Remapping and Rethinking African American Religion

1. Lewis Gordon, "Existential Dynamics of Theorizing Black Invisibility," in Gordon, ed., *Existence in Black: An Anthology of Black Existential Philosophy* (New York: Routledge, 1997), 72.

2. James Baldwin, *Go Tell It on the Mountain* (New York: Dell, 1953).

3. Ibid., 200–201.

4. Ibid., 201.

5. W. E. B. DuBois, *The Souls of Black Folk* (New York: Vintage, 1990), 7.

6. Baldwin, *Go Tell It on the Mountain*, 204.

7. Ibid., 221.

8. Clifton H. Johnson, ed., *God Struck Me Dead: Religious Conversion Experiences and Autobiographies of Ex-Slaves* (Philadelphia: Pilgrim, 1969), 45.

9. Ibid., 40–41.

10. Julia A. J. Foote, "A Brand Plucked from the Fire: An Autobiographical Sketch," in Williams L. Andrews, ed., *Sisters of the Spirit: Three Black Women's Autobiographies of the Nineteenth Century* (Bloomington: Indiana University Press, 1986), 174.

11. Ibid., 175.

12. Ibid., 176, 177.

13. Ibid., 180.

14. Ibid., 208.

15. E. U. Essien-Udom, *Black Nationalism: A Search for Identity in America* (Chicago: University of Chicago Press, 1962), 201.

16. C. Eric Lincoln, *The Black Muslims in America*, 3rd ed. (Grand Rapids: Eerdmans, 1994), 106.

17. Gayraud Wilmore, *Black Religion and Black Radicalism: An Interpretation of the Religious History of Afro-American People*, 2nd ed. (Maryknoll: Orbis, 1983).

18. Beverly Hall Lawrence, *Reviving the Spirit: A Generation of African Americans Goes Home to Church* (New York: Grove, 1996), 16.

19. Ibid., 28–29.

20. Edward P. Wimberly and Anne Streaty Wimberly, *Liberation and Human Wholeness: The Conversion Experiences of Black People in Slavery and Freedom* (Nashville: Abingdon, 1986), 16.

21. Ibid., 19.

22. Ibid., 22, 60.

23. Charles Long, "Prolegomenon to a Religious Herme-neutic," in *Significations: Signs, Symbols, and Images in the Interpretation of Religion* (Philadelphia: Fortress Press, 1986).

24. Ibid., 32.

25. Ibid., 46.

26. Ibid., 51.

27. Hilton Als, foreword to Deborah Chasman and Edna Chiang, eds., *Drawing Us In: How We Experience Visual Art* (Boston: Beacon, 2000), ix.

28. Arthur Danto, *After the End of Art: Contemporary Art and the Pale of History* (Princeton: Princeton University Press, 1995), 98.

29. Sharon Welch, *A Feminist Ethic of Risk* (Minneapolis: Fortress Press, 2000), 70.

30. Stuart Hall, "What Is This 'Black' in Black Popular Cul-ture?" in Michele Wallace and Gina Dent, ed., *Black Popular Culture* (New York: New, 1999), 29, 30.

Chapter 5: A New Theory of African American Religion

1. Mircea Eliade, *The Sacred and the Profane: The Nature of Religion* (New York: Harvest, 1959), 64.

2. Wayne L. Proudfoot, *Religious Experience* (Berkeley: Uni-versity of California Press, 1985), 155–227.

3. Proudfoot, *Religious Experience*, secs. 5 and 6; Ann Taves, *Fits, Trances and Visions: Experiencing Religion and Explainig Experience from Wesley to James* (Princeton: Prince-ton University Press, 1999), introduction and pt. 3.

4. Edward P. Wimberly and Anne Streaty Wimberly, *Lib-eration and Human Wholeness: The Conversion Experience of Black People in Slavery and Freedom* (Nashville: Abingdon, 1986), 19–21.

5. Ibid., 21.

6. Until recently the organization African Americans for Humanism (headed by Norm Allen until June 2010), based out of the Center for Free Inquiry, served as a hallmark of this non-religious orientation.

7. See for example Charles H. Long, *Significations: Signs, Symbols, and Images in the Interpretation of Religion* (Philadel-phia: Fortress Press, 1986).

8. Mirea Eliade and Joseph M. Kitagawa, eds., *The History of Religions: Essays in Methodology* (Chicago: University of Chicago Press, 1959), 97–98.

9. Arnold Hauser, "The Scope and Limitations of a Sociology of Art," in *The Philosophy of Art History* (London: Routledge, 1959), reprinted in Eric Fernie, ed., *Art History and Its Methods* (London: Phaidon, 1995), 205.

10. Jonathan Z. Smith, *Map Is Not Territory: Studies in the History of Religions* (Chicago: University of Chicago Press, 1993), 129, 130.

11. Ibid., 101.

12. Ibid., 291, 308.

For Further Reading

Atuama Nwokocha, Eziaku. *Vodou en Vogue: Fashioning Black Divinities in Haiti and the United States.* Chapel Hill: University of North Carolina Press, 2023.

Baer, Hans A. And Merrill Singer. *African-American Religion in the Twentieth Century: Varieties of Protest and Accommodation.* Knoxville: The University of Tennessee Press, 1992.

Cameron, Christopher and Phillip Luke Sinitiere, editors. *Race, Religion, and Black Lives Matter: Essays on a Moment and a Movement.* Nashville: Vanderbilt University Press, 2021.

Cannon, Katie. *Katie's Canon: Womanism and the Soul of the Black Community.* New York: Continuum, 1995.

Covington-Ware, Yolanda and Jeanette S. Jouili, editors. *Embodying Black Religion in African and Its Diasporas.* Durham: Duke University Press, 2021.

Crawley, Ashon T. *Blackpentecostal Breath: The Aesthetics of Possibility.* New York: Fordham University Press, 2016.

Curtis, Edward E. and Danielle Brune Sigler, editors. *The New Black Gods: Arthur Huff Fauset and the Study of African American*

Religions. Bloomington: Indiana University Press, 2009.

Essien-Udom, E. U. *Black Nationalism: Search for an Identity in America.* Chicago: The University of Chicago Press, 1995.

Ferguson, Leland. *Uncommon Ground: Archaeology and Early African America, 1650–1800.* Washington, D.C.: Smithsonian Institution Press, 1992.

Frederickson, George M. *The Black Image in the White Mind: The Debate on Afro-American Character and Destiny, 1817–1914.* New York: Harper & Row, 1971.

Gomez, Michael A. *Exchanging Our Country Marks: The Transformation of African Identities in the Colonial and Antebellum South.* Chapel Hill: The University of North Carolina Press, 1998.

Harris, Frederick. *Something Within: Religion in African-American Political Activism.* New York: Oxford University Press, 1999.

Hoel, Nina, Melissa Wilcox, Liz Wilson. *Religion, the Body, and Sexuality.* New York: Routledge, 2020.

Johnson, Sylvester A. *African American Religions, 1500-2000.* New York: Cambridge University Press, 2015.

Johnson, Terrence L. *We Testify with Our Lives: How Religion Transformed Radical Thought from Black Power to Black Lives Matter.* New York: Columbia University Press, 2021.

Jordan, Winthrop D. *White Over Black: American Attitudes Toward the Negro, 1550–1812.* Chapel Hill: The University of North Carolina Press, 1968.

Lincoln, C. Eric. *The Black Muslims in America.* 3rd Edition. Grand Rapids: Eerdmans, 1994.

Lomax, Tamura. *Jezebel Unhinged: Loosing the Black Female Body in Religion and Culture.* Durham: Duke University Press, 2018.

Pérez, Elizabeth. *Religion in the Kitchen: Cooking, Talking, and the Making of Black Atlantic Traditions.* New York: New York University Press, 2016.

Pitts, Walter F., Jr. *Old Ship of Zion: The Afro-Baptist Ritual in the African Diaspora.* New York: Oxford University Press, 1993.

Savage, Barbara Dianne. *Your Spirits Walk Beside Us: The Politics of Black Religion.* Cambridge: Harvard University Press, 2009.

Strongman, Roberto. *Queering Black Atlantic Religions: Transcorporeality in Candomble, Santeria, and Vodou.* Durham: Duke University Press, 2019.

Thurman, Howard. *The Luminous Darkness.* Richmond, Ind.: Friends United Press, 1989.

Tobin, Jacqueline L., and Raymond G. Dobard. *Hidden in Plain View: A Secret Story of Quilts and the Underground Railroad.* New York: Anchor, 2000.

Wayne White, Carol. *Black Lives and Sacred Humanity: Toward an African American*

Religious Naturalism. New York: Fordham University Press, 2016.

Weisenfeld, Judith. *New World A-Coming: Black Religion and Racial Identity during the Great Migration.* New York: New York University Press, 2017.

West, Cornel. *Prophesy Deliverance!: An Afro-American Revolutionary Christianity.* Philadelphia: Westminster, 1982.

White, Shane and Graham White. *Stylin': African American Expressive Culture from Its Beginnings to the Zoot Suit.* Ithaca: Cornell University Press, 1998.

Wilmore, Gayraud S. *Black Religion and Black Radicalism: An Interpretation of the Religious History of Afro-American People.* 2nd Edition. Maryknoll, N.Y.: Orbis, 1983.

Winters, Joseph R. *Hope Draped in Black: Race, Melancholy, and the Agony of Progress.* Durham: Duke University Press, 2016.